Simply Whidbey

A collection of regional recipes from
Whidbey Island, Washington

Laura Moore

Deborah Skinner

Illustrated by Margaret Livermore

SARATOGA PUBLISHERS

Additional copies may be purchased for retail price
plus $3.00 postage and handling per book.
For Washington delivery please include sales tax.

Saratoga Publishers
1581 West Links Way
Oak Harbor, Washington 98277

First Printing April 1991
Second Printing September 1991
Third Printing June 1992
Fourth Printing January 1993
Fifth Printing October 1993
Sixth Printing August 1994
Seventh Printing July 1995
Eighth Printing February 1996

Library of Congress Catalog No. 90-081675

ISBN 0-9628766-0-7

Printed in the United States of America.

It takes many people to make a simple idea become a finished product. We are grateful for the support, encouragement and advice proffered by family, friends and new acquaintances.

We owe a special "thank you" to the following people;

To Chris Skinner for his continual assistance and belief in our project from beginning to end.

To Justin and Paul, Allison, Courtney, Nicholas and Hans for their pride and patience in a project that took time away from them.

To Patti Pattee and Norman Sturdevant for their willingness to advise and edit.

To Margaret Livermore for capturing the essence of Whidbey Island on canvas.

To Janice Veal and Dawn Ashbach for heading us in the right direction throughout the project.

To the memory of Captain Steven A. Hazelrigg, U.S.N., for his enthusiastic support in a project he was unable to see to completion.

To our mothers, Jane O'Kelley and Peggy Moore, who through their example, instilled in us a love for entertaining and an appreciation for combining the best of friends and family with the best of food from our kitchens . . . the heart of our homes.

"Friends – They are kind to each other's
hopes. They cherish each other's dreams."

– Thoreau

Coming Ashore
Clinton

Contents

Introduction   9

Appetizers   13

Soups and Salads   37

Vegetables   71

Entrées   91

Seafood   117

Desserts   141

Breads and Brunch   171

Gifts from Your Kitchen   201

Tourist Information   220

Index   221

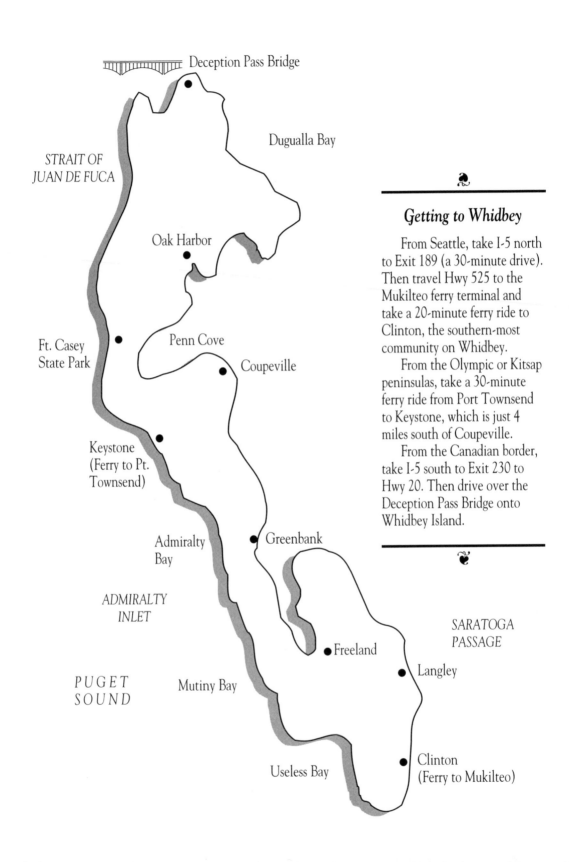

Deception Pass Bridge

Dugualla Bay

STRAIT OF
JUAN DE FUCA

Oak Harbor

Penn Cove

Ft. Casey
State Park

Coupeville

Keystone
(Ferry to Pt.
Townsend)

Admiralty
Bay

Greenbank

ADMIRALTY
INLET

SARATOGA
PASSAGE

Freeland

Langley

PUGET
SOUND

Mutiny Bay

Clinton
(Ferry to Mukilteo)

Useless Bay

Getting to Whidbey

From Seattle, take I-5 north to Exit 189 (a 30-minute drive). Then travel Hwy 525 to the Mukilteo ferry terminal and take a 20-minute ferry ride to Clinton, the southern-most community on Whidbey.

From the Olympic or Kitsap peninsulas, take a 30-minute ferry ride from Port Townsend to Keystone, which is just 4 miles south of Coupeville.

From the Canadian border, take I-5 south to Exit 230 to Hwy 20. Then drive over the Deception Pass Bridge onto Whidbey Island.

Introduction

Tucked away in the far northwestern corner of the United States lies an enchanting secret called Whidbey Island. Whidbey stretches 45 miles from Oak Harbor, Penn Cove and Coupeville in the north to Greenbank, Freeland, Langley and Clinton on the south end of the island. The landscape of this unusual island changes from the rolling farmlands of the north to the heavily timbered forests of the south. Whidbey's seclusion offers her visitors and residents opportunities for new adventures and new beginnings. From the moment you step foot onto her soil, you cannot help but sense the pioneer spirit that embodies this charming island; a spirit that began nearly 200 years ago.

On June 2, 1792, Captain George Vancouver landed at Penn Cove aboard the vessel *Discovery*. On a navigational mission four days later, First Mate Joseph Whidbey discovered the turbulent and narrow passage separating Whidbey Island from Fidalgo Island. Because of the churning waters and torrential currents, this passage appeared to be a river's inlet. Note of this discovery was brought back to Captain Vancouver who named this small passage between the two islands "Deception Pass." Captain Vancouver also named the island to the south "Whidbey's Island," after her discoverer, Joseph Whidbey.

According to local historians, the Skagit Indians were the first tribe to inhabit the island. They settled around the north end of the island, along with the neighboring Swinomish tribe. The Suquamish and Snohomish tribes dwelt on South Whidbey. Each of these tribes were dependent upon canoes for transportation and for the gathering of fish. For nearly 56 years, Whidbey served as a trading post between Indian inhabitants and the Spanish, British, American and Russian traders. In addition to trading with the Indians, many attempts were made by the traders to convert them to the Christian religion. The establishment of the Catholic mission, "Whitby," accompanied Whidbey's first legal land claim by settler Thomas Glasgow. Soon, new settlers arrived bringing hopes and dreams embodied in a pioneer spirit. It was during the 1850s that a small number of Irish settlers laid claim to Whidbey. These early Irish settlers farmed, sold general merchandise, and took an active role in local government. They were also very friendly with the local Indians and became known as their "white brothers."

There was a lull in settlement until 1894 when 18 Dutch colonists landed, via steamship, at San de Fuca of Whidbey. They were a hardy and venturesome bunch. The Dutch settlers brought with them a new language and a drive to prosper. Within two years there were over 200 Hollanders building their dreams on North Whidbey. Many of the homes, farms and businesses they built are still thriving today.

Noticeable growth and settlement of South Whidbey began in the 1880s. By 1900, nearly 500 persons were living on South Whidbey. The leading industry was not farming, but logging. The north and south ends of Whidbey functioned almost entirely as two separate communities. It wasn't until 1902 that the first county road was in place linking Coupeville, the county seat, with Langley. Until that time, access between the two regions was gained by boat or by walking 30 or 40 miles along the beach. The county road made trade and communication between North and South Whidbey a profitable affair.

In the early 1900s a sternwheeler ship served as the transportation link between Seattle and Oak Harbor, Coupeville, Langley and Clinton. The ship would leave Oak Harbor early each morning and complete the round trip by evening. Transporting a vehicle to and from the island was not possible until 1915 when the "Deception Pass" ferry made its way from Cornet Bay on Whidbey to a small beach on Fidalgo Island. This method of transport continued until July, 1935. It was at this time that Deception Pass bridge opened as the "gateway" to Whidbey Island.

In the late 1930s, the United States government purchased several hundred acres of farm land in the Clover Valley and Crescent Harbor areas of North Whidbey. The naval base contributed to an economic and population boom that caused the town of Oak Harbor to triple in size between 1940 and 1946. Navy families, past and present, have found Whidbey Island to be a glorious place. As a result, many have settled permanently on the island.

Whidbey Island is home to a variety of working people. Coupeville and Langley, for instance, provide a special haven for the arts. In addition, Whidbey serves as an "escape" from the bustling King County area. People living on the island and working in Seattle and Everett enjoy a daily ferry ride as they commute from South Whidbey to Mukilteo. Although the logging industry has slowed in recent years, farming continues to provide a steady occupation for many. Farming encompasses the harvesting of fruits and vegetables, dairy products and commercial shellfish.

Tourism on Whidbey is an industry that continues to grow each year. Visitors come to explore the local sights and take advantage of the many accommodations available from the Bed and Breakfast Inns to the State parks. Whidbey Island has also provided a quiet retreat for summer residents.

Whidbey Island has something for everyone. Whether you come for a day's visit or decide to lay down your roots, you'll be captivated by her serene, yet spirited atmosphere. The islanders of Whidbey, both young and old, share in the daily celebration of life that Whidbey offers. Take time to stroll along her beaches. Smell the sea air and imagine times gone by. Let her breezes whisper in your ear. Share her pioneer spirit. Whidbey is an island of simplistic, yet opulent character. Her flavor is what you desire – "Simply Whidbey."

Dedicated to all who appreciate the charm of Whidbey . . .

Brad P. Zylstra

Brad P. Zylstra

Captain Whidbey Inn
Coupeville

"Where the Waves of Juan de Fuca Kiss the Sands of Whidbey Isle"

"In the land of the golden sunset;
Where the Ku-ri-Si-wo flows;
You will find an Isle of beauty;
Bathed in sunshine and repose."

"Meet me, sweetheart, meet me with a smile,
Where the waves of Juan de Fuca,
Kiss the sands of Whidbey Isle."

"Moonbeams dance on rippled waters;
Zephyrs play on shimmering cove;
Mountains glisten in the sunshine;
Jewels in the scenes we love."

"Meet me, sweetheart, meet me with a smile,
Where the waves of Juan de Fuca,
Kiss the sands of Whidbey Isle;
Oh, meet me, sweetheart, meet me with a smile,
Where the waves of Juan de Fuca,
Kiss the sands of Whidbey Isle."

Words and Music by James Zylstra
Copyright ©1932

Smoked Salmon and Onion Cheesecake

3 1/2 (8 ounce) packages cream cheese at
    room temperature
4 large eggs
1/3 cup heavy cream
3 tablespoons butter plus butter for greasing
    the pan
1/3 cup fine bread crumbs
1/4 cup plus 3 tablespoons freshly grated
    Parmesan cheese
1/2 cup chopped onion
1/2 cup chopped green pepper
1/3 pound Nova Scotia salmon (prefer
    Portlock salmon)
1/2 cup Gruyère cheese
salt and pepper to taste

The *Captain Whidbey Inn*, built in 1907, is a madrona log inn situated on the wooded shores of Penn Cove. Smoked Salmon and Onion Cheesecake is often served as a first course in their charming dining room.

Your friends will appreciate your time and effort spent preparing this delectable dish.

Place the cream cheese, eggs and heavy cream in the bowl of an electric mixer. Beat the ingredients until thoroughly blended and quite smooth.

Butter the inside of a metal cheesecake pan 8 inches wide and 3 inches deep. Sprinkle the inside with the bread crumbs combined with 1/4 cup Parmesan cheese. Shake the crumbs around the bottom and sides until coated. Shake out the excess crumbs.

Sauté the onion and green pepper in 3 tablespoons of butter. Cut the salmon into small pieces.

Preheat the oven to 300°.

Fold the salmon, Gruyère cheese, remaining 3 tablespoons Parmesan cheese and sautéed onion and green pepper into the basic cheesecake mixture. Add salt and pepper to taste. Pour the batter into the prepared pan and shake gently to level the mixture.

Set the pan in a slightly larger pan and pour boiling water into the larger pan to a depth of 2 inches. Do not let the edges of the pans touch. Bake for 1 hour and 40 minutes. At the end of that time, turn off the oven heat and let the cake sit in the oven 1 hour longer. Lift the cake out of its water bath and place it on a rack to cool for at least 2 hours before unmolding. Place a round cake plate over the cake and carefully turn both upside down to unmold.

Cut into wedges and serve with an assortment of crackers.

24 servings

Seabolt's
Smoked Salmon Pâté

1/4 pound cream cheese
1/4 pound smoked salmon
1 tablespoon lemon juice
1/2 tablespoon minced onion
1/2 tablespoon minced parsley
1/4 teaspoon garlic powder

Mix all ingredients and thin with a little mayonnaise or lemon juice.

Serve the pâté with crackers.

Yield: 1 1/2 cups

A trip through the Deception Pass state park is not complete without sampling "Smoked Salmon Pâté" at *Seabolt's*. Jim has smoked salmon of different varieties, and he smokes turkey, chicken and beef. The salmon jerky is a real treat for a passing visitor.

Seabolt's
Smoked Salmon Antipasto

Proprietor Jim Seabolt packs and sends Whidbey Island smoked salmon to customers around the world. He highly recommends this recipe for a delightful hors d'oeuvre.

Arrange slices of smoked salmon, mozzarella cheese and avocado on a platter. Drizzle with vinaigrette dressing and serve with warm crusty bread.

The word antipasto literally means "before the meal." It refers to a light snack to be served quickly and easily in order to stimulate the appetite.

Whidbey Fish Mussels

2/3 cup olive oil
1/2 teaspoon oregano
1/2 teaspoon basil
4 pounds fresh Penn Cove mussels
1/2 cup red wine vinegar
1/4 cup white wine
1/4 cup butter, melted

In a large pot, heat olive oil over medium high heat. When the oil is hot, add oregano and basil. Spoon the mussels into the hot oil. Cover the pot and allow the mussels to cook until their shells open (usually 3 to 5 minutes).

When the mussels have opened, sprinkle them with red wine vinegar. Cover the pot and cook for 1 minute. Pour white wine and butter over the mussels and stir carefully to coat all the mussels with broth.

Serve mussels in bowls of hot broth with plenty of crusty French bread for dunking.

8 servings

The informal atmosphere at *Whidbey Fish*, in Greenbank, is inviting to any island wanderer. It's a great fresh fish market and a delightful cafe serving the catch of the day. Plan to spend some time visiting with the owner, Thom Gunn, and perusing his unusual memorabilia. He recommends the following method of preparing mussels.

There are two mussel farms on the waters of Penn Cove: Penn Cove Mussels and West Coast Blue Mussels. Between the two businesses around 3/4 million pounds of mussels are harvested each year. The mussels grow on ropes in the water that are connected to the mussel rafts. Harvest begins in early spring and continues throughout November, or as late as February. Penn Cove mussels are found on menus across the United States.

Turkish Fried Mussels

1 package dried yeast
1/8 teaspoon sugar
1 cup flour
2 1/2 tablespoons butter, melted
1/8 teaspoon salt
2 eggs, separated
30 large mussels
1/2 cup white wine (optional)
1 cup flour
oil for deep frying

Dissolve the yeast in a bowl of 1/2 cup water. Add sugar. Set the bowl in a warm place for 10 minutes until yeast begins to foam.

Sift the flour into a large bowl. Add melted butter, salt and egg yolks and mix together well. Beat the egg whites until stiff.

While stirring constantly, add the yeast mixture to the flour. The batter should be fairly liquid. Allow the mixture to rise in a warm place for 1 hour. Fold in the egg whites.

Wash mussels under tap water and remove the "beards," seaweed and barnacles. Throw away any broken or open shells. Place mussels in a large pan with 1/2 cup water or the wine. Season them lightly with salt, according to your taste, and bring the water to a boil. Cover and allow water to boil until shells open, about 4 minutes.

Remove mussels from their shells and pat them dry on a clean cloth. Heat oil in a deep frying pan. Roll the mussels quickly in flour, dip in batter and drop 3 or 4 at a time into hot oil. Fry for 1 minute until crisp and brown.

Serve immediately with or without our Lemon Herb Sauce, found on page 83.

6 servings

Greek and Continental cuisine reign at *Café Langley*. Shant and Arshaver Garibyan use local mussels in an innovative and delicious manner.

We suggest dipping the fried mussels in our Lemon Herb Sauce.

Clams on the Half Shell

2 pounds little neck butter clams, scrubbed

1 egg

1 tablespoon milk

2/3 cup flour

2 teaspoons chopped parsley

1 teaspoon basil

1 teaspoon garlic salt

1 teaspoon grated lemon peel

1/2 teaspoon pepper

2 tablespoons oil

2 tablespoons butter

lemon wedges

Steam clams in 2 cups water for 3 minutes or until all shells have opened. Drain. Remove the top shell from each clam by cutting the muscle which holds the shell closed. Discard the top half of the shell.

In a shallow dish, beat the egg and milk together. In another shallow dish, mix flour, parsley, basil, garlic salt, lemon peel, and pepper.

In a large skillet heat oil and butter over medium high heat. Dip clam shells in the egg mixture and then in the flour. Place the clam and shell in hot skillet, clam side down, and fry for 3 minutes. Drain on paper towels before serving.

Arrange the clams on a serving platter with lemon wedges.

8 servings

The best time of year for low tides on Whidbey Island is early summer. It's always fun to grab pails, shovels and boots and head for the beach in search of a variety of local clams. The following clam recipe is great for an informal gathering of family and friends.

Shellfish around Whidbey Island are sometimes affected by paralytic shellfish poisoning, also known as Red Tide. Red Tide is caused by poisonous single-celled organisms that live in salt water. Shellfish, such as clams and oysters, and other bivalve species take in the organisms; thus they become affected by Red Tide. The human digestive system will also react to the shellfish poisoning. To find out if there is a Red Tide alert and where the Red Tide is, contact the Red Tide Hotline at 1-800-526-5632.

Escargot in Mushroom Caps

1 cup butter, divided
24 very large, firm mushroom caps
1/3 cup finely chopped parsley
2 cloves garlic, minced
3 tablespoons finely chopped green onion
1 tablespoon lemon juice
dash of nutmeg
2 (4 1/2 ounces, each) cans snails, drained
4 tablespoons fresh bread crumbs
2 tablespoons orange liqueur
parsley for garnish

Preheat oven to 400°.

In a large skillet, melt 3 tablespoons of butter. Add the mushrooms and sauté them until lightly brown. Remove from pan and drain on paper towels. Cream the remaining butter with parsley, garlic, green onion, lemon juice and nutmeg. Fill the mushroom caps with the butter mixture. Place a snail in each mushroom cap and drizzle 1 teaspoon of the remaining butter over each.

Mix bread crumbs with orange liqueur and top each stuffed mushroom with 1/2 teaspoonful of the bread mixture. Bake the finished product in a 400° oven 10 to 15 minutes. The bread crumbs should be golden and the butter bubbly before you remove them.

Serve immediately on a tray garnished with parsley.

24 Escargot

Don't let the unique nature of escargot discourage you from trying this elegant and tasty appetizer. Catherine Dunn serves thin baguette slices along with the mushroom caps to absorb any leftover garlic butter.

Warm Crab Dip

1 (8 ounce) package cream
   cheese, softened at room
   temperature
1/4 cup milk
1 tablespoon mayonnaise
2 tablespoons chili sauce
3 drops tabasco sauce
2 tablespoons minced onion
1/2 teaspoon dry mustard

1/4 teaspoon salt
1 cup cooked crab (such as
   Dungeness)
3 tablespoons sliced green
   olives
1 (8 1/2 ounce) can
   artichokes (not
   marinated), coarsely
   chopped

Preheat oven to 375°.

In a mixing bowl, combine all ingredients except crab, the
olives and artichokes. Mix thoroughly. Gently fold in the
remaining ingredients. Spread into an 8-inch baking dish.

Bake at 375° for 15 minutes.

Serve Crab Dip, while hot, along with crackers or corn chips.

8 servings

U.S. Senator Slade Gorton
is a frequent visitor to Whidbey
Island, the location of his
family's summer home. Senator
Gorton sent us one of his
favorite appetizer recipes. The
dish has notable "Northwest
character."

Crab Deviled Eggs

6 whole eggs, hard boiled
1 cup fresh crabmeat, or
   1 (8 ounce) can crabmeat
1 cup finely diced celery

1 tablespoon French salad
   dressing
1/3 cup sour cream

After allowing the eggs to cool, slice eggs in half (lengthwise)
and remove yolks. You may want to mash the yolks and add
them to the filling. Otherwise, combine crabmeat, celery, salad
dressing and sour cream. Blend well. Refill the egg halves.

Cover the eggs with plastic wrap and refrigerate until serving.

12 eggs

Deviled eggs are always a
welcome treat at any barbeque
or picnic. Kay Roodzant uses
crab in this recipe to produce
deviled eggs with a Northwest
flair.

Steak Tartare

1 1/4 pounds freshly ground sirloin steak
    or tenderloin, chilled

1 egg

1/3 cup finely chopped white onion

3 tablespoons chopped parsley

1 clove garlic, minced

1 tablespoon Dijon mustard

1 teaspoon grated horseradish

1 tablespoon worcestershire sauce

Garnish:

2 tablespoons capers

2 tablespoons chopped tomatoes

2 tablespoons chopped green onion

2 tablespoons chopped olives

Cocktail size bread slices

It may be helpful to have your butcher grind the meat lean.
It should be put through the grinder several times. Then,
mix steak, egg, onion, parsley, garlic, mustard, horseradish
and worcestershire sauce in a large bowl. Chill until serving.

To serve, mound the steak mixture on a plate lined with a
bed of lettuce. Circle the mound with the garnishes. Steak
Tartare is spread on small rounds of bread and sprinkled
with garnishes.

10 servings

Introduce this sophisticated
snack sensation to your guests
accompanied with a glass of
bold red wine. We recommend
Ste. Michelle Cabernet
Sauvignon.

*European cooks add parsley
to their food almost as easily as
American cooks add salt to their
food.*

Beef Teriyaki

1 pound beef round steak
1/4 cup soy sauce
1 tablespoon sherry
1 tablespoon sugar
1/2 teaspoon ginger
1/4 teaspoon garlic powder

Begin preparation of this dish by placing the meat in your freezer. When it is nearly frozen, slice it into thin strips.

In a small bowl, mix all ingredients except steak. Place meat in a deep bowl and pour marinade over. Stir to coat all meat slices. Allow meat to marinate for 30 minutes at room temperature.

Thread marinated slices of meat on skewers (accordian style) and broil or grill 4 inches from heat for 1 to 2 minutes on each side.

24 skewers

To attractively serve Beef Teriyaki, insert the skewers of beef into a halved melon. Add fruit kabobs to the melon half as an appealing accompaniment.

An appetizer is anything that inspires a desire or relish for food.

– Charles H. Baker

Appetizing Mini Quiche

1 box Pillsbury All Ready pie crust containing
   2 crusts

6 eggs

3 slices bacon, cooked crisp and crumbled

1/3 cup shredded Swiss cheese

salt and pepper to taste

1 teaspoon Dijon style mustard

1/2 cup heavy cream or half and half

1/3 cup sour cream and parsley sprigs for garnish

Preheat oven to 350°. Spray mini muffin pans with a natural cooking spray.

Unfold the crusts as directed on package. Using a 2 or 2 1/2 inch cookie cutter, cut 12 to 15 rounds from each crust. Gently place a round in each muffin cup and push down to form a small hollow crust. Prick each crust with a fork 3 or 4 times. Bake empty crusts 10 minutes at 350°. Crusts should be lightly browned, yet firm enough to retain their shape. Cool thoroughly on a wire rack. At this point the miniature crusts may be frozen in a single layer and stored in an airtight container until needed.

Beat eggs in a large bowl. Add bacon, cheese, salt, pepper, and mustard. Mix in the heavy cream or half and half. Place 1 teaspoon of filling in each crust. Place in oven on center rack at 350° for 20 minutes. Bake until golden brown and firm. Cool on wire rack.

When ready to use the frozen pre-cooked crusts, fill each one and bake as directed above.

Garnish each quiche with sour cream and parsley sprigs. Serve at room temperature.

30 pieces

Cheryl May finds this super quick appetizer handy for use in her catering business, *A Catered Affair.* Make these mini crusts ahead and freeze them until you are ready to use them. Cheryl likes to garnish each "mini quiche" with sour cream stars and parsley sprigs.

Spicy Chile Cheese Squares

4 (4 ounce) cans whole green chiles
2 pounds Monterey Jack cheese, grated
5 eggs
1 (13 ounce) can evaporated milk
1 1/2 tablespoons flour
salt and pepper to taste

Preheat oven to 350°.

Split chiles in half and remove seeds.

In a 9 x 13-inch pan, layer half the chiles and half of the cheese; repeat.

Mix all other ingredients and pour over chiles and cheese.

Bake at 350° for 35-45 minutes until firm in center. Let the pan stand 10 minutes before cutting into squares and serving.

Serve Spicy Chile Cheese Squares with cocktails in the evening. They are also delightful served as part of a luncheon or brunch.

20 squares

Rosemary Toft has done a lot of entertaining during her years as a Navy spouse. She provides us with a warm appetizer that can be cut into small squares.

The Whidbey Island Naval Air Station is located on 4,360 acres in Oak Harbor on North Whidbey. The naval air station supports naval aviation forces and provides approximately 46 percent of Island County's population. About 24,400 people are employees and dependents of the base.

Stuffed Cheese Puffs

2 cups grated sharp cheese
1/2 cup butter, softened
1 cup flour
1/2 teaspoon salt

1 teaspoon paprika
1 (6 ounce) jar stuffed green
   olives, or
6 ounces pepperoni

Preheat oven to 400°.

Cream the cheese and butter together. Add flour, salt and paprika to cheese mixture and blend it well.

If you are using pepperoni as the stuffing, cut it into bite size pieces that will fit in the middle of 1 tablespoon cheese mixture. Otherwise, use 1 tablespoon of cheese mixture to form a ball around the olives.

Bake at 400° for 15 minutes and serve while hot.

36 puffs

The cheese puffs will freeze well if laid out on a baking sheet to "flash freeze." Wrap them tightly in foil or use freezer bags for storage.

Creamy Garlic Cheese

1 (8 ounce) package cream
   cheese or Neufchatel
   cheese
2 tablespoons garlic, minced
1 teaspoon thyme

1/4 teaspoon salt
1/8 teaspoon ground black
   pepper
1/2 cup heavy cream

Allow the cheese to come to room temperature. In a small mixing bowl, stir the cheese until it is soft. Add the garlic, thyme, salt and pepper; stir until thoroughly combined.

In a separate bowl, whip the cream until it holds stiff peaks. Stir half the whipped cream into the cheese; then fold in the other half of the whipped cream. Try to retain as much volume as possible.

Pack the cheese in an airtight container and keep refrigerated.

Yield 1 1/2 cups

The following recipe is simple, but the flavor is memorable. It is the perfect complement to use with Stuffed Chicken Breasts, as a spread on crackers or a tasty filling in broiled mushroom caps.

Cheddar Asparagus Roll-Ups

20 asparagus spears
3/4 cup butter or margarine, softened
1 tablespoon fresh chopped parsley
1/2 teaspoon dill weed
3 tablespoons chopped green onion
salt and pepper to taste
6-8 ounces sharp cheddar cheese
1 loaf sliced bread

Discard the white fibrous ends from the asparagus and rinse spears. Bring about 1 inch water to boil in a wide, shallow pan; drop asparagus in water and boil uncovered. Cook until tender when pierced, about 4-7 minutes. Drain well.

In a small bowl combine 1/2 cup of the butter, parsley, dill, onion, and salt and pepper. Set aside.

Cut cheese into sticks 2 1/2 to 3 inches long and 1/4 to 1/2 inch in width.

Trim crusts from 20 bread slices and flatten each slice slightly with a rolling pin.

Spread butter mixture evenly over 1 side of each bread slice and top each with an asparagus spear and a cheese stick. Roll each bread slice around asparagus and cheese and secure with a wooden pick. Arrange on a baking sheet.

Melt the remaining 1/4 cup butter and brush evenly over rolls. Broil rolls about 5 inches from heat until golden, for about 4 minutes, turning once.

Serve while warm.

20 pieces

Appetizers should be fresh and imaginative. Sharon Solin enjoys serving this because of its variety of texture, color and flavor.

"Many's the long night I've dreamed of cheese – toasted mostly."

– Robert Louis Stevenson

Spinach Turnovers

1 teaspoon dry yeast
1/2 cup olive oil
7 cups flour
1 1/2 teaspoon salt
Spinach filling

Dissolve yeast in 1 tablespoon of warm water. Stir in oil and the flour mixed with salt. Add enough cold water (1/4 cup at a time) to make a stiff dough. Cover and let stand 30 minutes.

Preheat oven to 375°.

Roll dough out on floured board to 1/4 inch thickness. Cut in circles with a biscuit cutter measuring 4 inches in diameter. Put a tablespoon of filling on each pastry round. Bring the edges up into a triangular shape and press these edges together firmly. Place on a greased cookie sheet.

Bake at 375° for 20 minutes or until lightly browned.

Spinach filling

2 pounds fresh spinach, stems removed
1/2 cup olive oil
1 cup chopped onion
1 cup pine nuts
2 tablespoons lemon juice
1/2 teaspoon ground sumac, (optional)
salt and pepper to taste

Wash and dry the spinach. Chop it finely. Mix all the ingredients together. For full flavor, allow the filling to set for 15 minutes before filling the pastries.

50 turnovers

This is one of Laura's favorite recipes she collected while living in the Middle East. Lebanese cooks place these pastries on round trays and carry them to the local bakery to be cooked. Their hot bakery ovens produce a light, flaky crust.

Sumac is a Mediterranean seasoning and is available at delicatessens featuring Greek, Middle Eastern or Mediterranean foods and spices.

Button Mushroom Dip

1/2 cup butter

2 cloves garlic, minced

2 tablespoons worcestershire sauce

7 (4 ounce) cans whole button mushrooms

fresh ground pepper to taste

1 (16 ounce) container sour cream

1 teaspoon garlic powder

salt to taste

In a saucepan melt butter over medium heat. Add garlic and worcestershire. Drain 6 cans of mushrooms, reserving 1 can of juice. Add the reserved mushroom juice and ground pepper to butter mixture. Spoon the mushrooms into the saucepan and allow them to simmer and soak in the seasoning. Keep them on low heat for at least 1 hour, making sure that mushrooms remain hot.

In a small serving dish mix the sour cream, garlic powder and salt. Liberally add more garlic to the sour cream if desired.

Serve the mushrooms, with or without their butter sauce, along with the sour cream. Set out cocktail forks or picks with which to dip the mushrooms in the sour cream.

8 servings

If you like the taste of mushrooms and garlic you will certainly enjoy this appetizer. Jane O'Kelley presents the mushrooms in a fondue pot, thereby allowing them to simmer in the butter sauce.

Pepper first appeared in Sanskrit medical records 3,000 years ago. It is made from round berries off an evergreen climbing vine that is native to the jungles of the Malabar Coast of southwest India. Those nations that produce pepper export more than 2,000,000,000 pounds annually.

Pepper is the most commonly used spice.

Bacon Stuffed Mushrooms

1 dozen large mushrooms
3/4 pound bacon
3/4 cup grated cheddar cheese
1/2 cup chopped green onion
2 tablespoons olive oil

Wash the mushrooms, remove their stems and drain on a paper towel.

Fry the bacon until crisp and drain it. When cool, crumble the cooked bacon into small pieces. Mix bacon together with cheese and green onions.

Brush mushrooms lightly with olive oil. Place 2-3 teaspoons of bacon mixture in the hollow of each mushroom. Place mushrooms on a broiler pan. They may be refrigerated for several hours.

Preheat oven to broil.

Place stuffed mushrooms under hot broiler and broil 2 to 3 minutes or until the cheese bubbles.

Serve the mushrooms immediately.

12 mushrooms

The ingredients for stuffed mushrooms are often readily at hand which makes this a great appetizer for unexpected guests.

Early Egyptian pharaohs reserved mushrooms for royal use only.

Continental Cheese Fondue

1 pound Gruyère cheese, shredded
3 tablespoons flour
2 cups light, dry, white wine
salt, pepper and nutmeg to taste
2 tablespoons brandy
2 cloves garlic, minced

Dredge shredded cheese with flour. Pour the wine in the pot and heat slowly in a double boiler. When the wine is heated to the point that air bubbles rise to the surface, but is not boiling, stir with a fork and add cheese a handful at a time.

Stir constantly after each addition, making sure that all cheese is dissolved before another handful is added. Continue stirring until mixture starts bubbling. Add salt, pepper and nutmeg to taste. Stir in brandy.

Rub a chafing dish with minced garlic.

Pour cheese fondue into the chafing dish and set over low flame. Care should be taken that the fondue keeps bubbling lightly by regulating the flame.

Bread should be cut into bite size pieces, each of which must have at least 1 side of crust.

Encourage your friends to spear a piece of bread with a fork, piercing the soft part of the bread first and securing the point of the fork in the crust. Bread should be dunked in a stirring motion, one diner after the other, to help maintain the proper consistency of fondue. If, towards the end of the meal, some of the melted cheese should form a brown crust at the bottom of the utensil, lift the crust out of the bottom of the dish with a fork. This crust is considered a delicacy.

6 servings

Rick Almberg convinced us that his neighbor, Mary Bradt, knew the secret for delicious fondue. Try this recipe as an intimate beginning to a formal dinner.

Traditionally there is a price to pay for losing one's bread in the fondue pot. The guilty party must forfeit a turn, buy the next bottle of wine or kiss the person of his choice at the table.

Vegetable Cheese Spread

1 cup (4 ounces) farmer cheese

3 tablespoons plain yogurt

1 teaspoon lemon juice

1 teaspoon soy sauce

1/4 cup chopped apple

1/4 cup chopped carrot

2 tablespoons finely chopped celery

2 tablespoons chopped pecans

2 tablespoons raisins or currants

1 tablespoon toasted wheat germ

1/2 teaspoon curry powder

pita bread

Preheat oven to broil.

In a food processor blend the cheese, yogurt, lemon juice, and soy sauce. Stir in, or briefly process, the remaining ingredients. Spread cheese mixture on split pita breads and cut into wedges. Broil in the oven for 3 minutes.

Serve wedges on a tray garnished with fresh parsley sprigs.

Yield: 2 cups

Savor this sophisticated version of a cheese log or ball. Tina Salter's bountiful spread contains an array of vegetables and fruits making it an appealing and unusual hors d'oeuvre.

Hot Artichoke Spread

1 (8 1/2 ounce) can artichoke hearts, drained
1 (16 ounce) jar marinated artichoke hearts, drained
1 (4 ounce) can diced green chiles
6 tablespoons mayonnaise
1 1/2 cups cheddar cheese, grated

Preheat oven to 350°.

Chop the artichoke hearts (from the can) into small pieces and spread in a medium size baking dish. Chop the artichoke hearts (from the jar) and spread them on top of the first layer of artichokes. Scatter the chiles over the artichokes. Spread the mayonnaise over the chiles as the fourth layer. Sprinkle the grated cheese on top.

Bake at 350° for 15 minutes.

Serve with tortilla chips, crackers or toasted pita chips.

8 servings

Not only will your friends ask for more artichoke cheese dip, they'll ask you for the recipe as well.

Pita Chips

6 rounds pita bread
3/4 cup butter, melted
1 1/2 tablespoons grated Parmesan cheese

Preheat oven to 350°.

Divide each pita into 2 rounds by carefully inserting a knife into the edge and cutting around the circumference of the hollow bread. Brush each of the 12 halves with melted butter and sprinkle with 1 tablespoon cheese. Slice the rounds into 8 pie shaped pieces and place them in a single layer on an ungreased baking sheet, (cheese side up).

Bake at 350° for 12 to 15 minutes.

Serve while warm or store for several days in a plastic bag.

48 chips

Try these crisp chips as an alternative to potato or tortilla chips.

Fiesta Bean Dip

1 (10 1/2 ounce) container bean dip

1 cup sour cream

1/2 package taco seasoning

1 tablespoon salsa

10-20 drops tabasco, according to taste

1 (8 ounce) package cream cheese

1/2 cup grated cheddar cheese

1/2 cup grated Monterey Jack cheese

Mix the bean dip, sour cream, taco seasoning, salsa, and tabasco. Cube the cream cheese and blend into bean dip mixture. Microwave on high for 4-5 minutes. Top with grated cheeses. Cover dish with a lid and microwave once more until most of the cheese melts on top of the bean dip.

Serve with tortilla chips.

Yield: 3 cups

The cheeses in this Mexican appetizer make it particularly creamy. Put this dip in a covered casserole dish and cook it in your microwave. Melissa and Brad Zylstra believe this is one recipe that will be used again and again.

Sangria

3 oranges	3 lemons
3 apples	1 fifth burgandy wine
3 limes	5 ounces Triple Sec liqueur

Wash and slice all fruit. In a large serving pitcher or container add the burgandy and liqueur to the fruit. Blend well and refrigerate for 2 days. Stir occasionally.

Remove the fruit from the pitcher before serving individual glasses of Sangria over ice. Garnish each serving with an orange wedge.

6 servings

Create a fiesta!

Guacamole Dip

2 garlic cloves, minced
1 medium onion
2 tomatoes
2 avocados
1/2 teaspoon salt
1/2 tablespoon lemon juice
dash of tabasco
chopped tomato pieces for garnish

Process all ingredients.

Garnish the top of your Guacamole Dip with chopped tomato pieces.

Yield: 1 1/2 cups

This is a recipe you can use as a starting point for creating your own original guacamole dip. Good luck!

Placing an avocado in a plastic bag with a few strips of banana peel will hasten ripening.

Taco Salsa

1 (28 ounce) can diced tomatoes
12 jalapeño peppers, chopped
4 medium onions, chopped
2 cups white vinegar
2 teaspoons ground black pepper
1 (8 ounce) can tomato sauce, optional

Adjust the number of jalapeños used for milder or spicier salsa. Combine all ingredients and simmer over low heat for 2 1/2 to 3 hours.

To store salsa put it in a tightly covered container and store in the refrigerator or freezer.

Yield: 2 cups

Try Van Westfall's tried and true version of salsa. Van uses fresh jalapeños. Beware – it's hot!

Egg Nog

12 eggs, separated
3/4 cup sugar
1 quart milk
1 1/2 teaspoons vanilla
1/2 gallon vanilla ice
  cream, softened

1 quart heavy cream,
  whipped
1 teaspoon each nutmeg,
  cinnamon, mace, cloves
brandy, optional

The holiday season
brings to mind warm feelings
for friends, traditions and
extended hospitality. These
rich beverages will establish a
tradition to be repeated year
after year.

In a large bowl beat the egg yolks with 1/4 cup sugar until
light and fluffy. Add milk and vanilla to yolk mixture. Fold
in softened ice cream. Add 1/2 cup sugar to whipped cream
and fold into yolk mixture. Beat the egg whites until stiff. Stir
the whites into the egg nog mixture along with the spices.

To each serving add 1 jigger brandy, a dollop of whipped
cream and a dash of freshly grated nutmeg. Or, try Egg Nog
prepared the way the folks at Whidbey's Greenbank Farm
suggest. Add 1 ounce Whidbeys liqueur to each mug and top
with whipped cream and nutmeg.

12 servings

Hot Buttered Rum

1/2 pound brown sugar
1/4 pound butter
1 pint vanilla ice cream

grated nutmeg and whole
  cinnamon sticks for
  garnish

In a large saucepan melt the brown sugar and butter together
over medium heat. Add the ice cream and blend well. Store
the mix in the freezer in a tightly covered container.

When ready to serve Hot Buttered Rum to guests, use 4
teaspoons of mix in each large mug. Add 1 1/2 jiggers rum and
fill the mug with boiling water. Blend thoroughly and serve
immediately.

Garnish individual Hot Buttered Rums with freshly grated
nutmeg and a cinnamon stick.

Yield: 4 cups

City Beach Windmill
Oak Harbor

Fort Casey Picnic and Beachcombing

Each year about a half million visitors explore Central Whidbey's Fort Casey. Overlooking western Puget Sound, the fort is on land that was purchased by the government in the early 1950s. A 137-acre state park was established to preserve the concrete fort and the miles of tunnels that surround this structure. The complex was operational during both world wars and supported a bakery, post office, two saloons, a bowling alley, a hospital and barracks. Today the fort is extremely popular with those who love to fly kites, picnic, beachcomb, camp, explore, attend recreational summer camps, swim and experience a bit of history firsthand. Park information: 678-4519.

Smoked Salmon and Onion Cheesecake

Vicchysoisse

Baguettes with French Herb Butter

Vegetables with Mint Marinade

Whidbeys Berry Pie

Evening Boat Cruise through Penn Cove

Archaeologists have estimated that the population of Penn Cove two hundred years ago equals that of the current population of the area. Due to the bounty received from land crops, fish, shellfish and edible plants, Penn Cove was an important gathering place. It was also a place of celebration where Indians and early Whidbey settlers held "potlatches" and took part in annual canoe races. Penn Cove continues to provide an abundance of foods harvested from the salty bay and the rich soil left by melting glaciers.

Chilled Vegetable Soup

Oyster Sauce Beef

Artichoke Caesar Salad

Stir Fried Snap Peas

Strawberry Peach Delight

Tomato Beef Vegetable Soup

2 pounds stew meat

1 large yellow onion, chopped

1 1/4 teaspoons pepper

1 teaspoon seasoned salt

5 medium carrots

5 stalks celery

4 medium size potatoes

1 cup frozen green beans

1 (28 ounce) can tomatoes, cut up

2 packages au jus mix

3 bay leaves

In a large kettle brown stew meat with onions, pepper and salt. Add 4 cups water to the kettle. Bring to a boil; turn down heat and simmer soup 40 minutes.

Cut the carrots, celery and potatoes into small 1/2 inch pieces. Add all vegetables, au jus mixes, and bay leaves to the soup. Mix in 3 more cups water and bring soup to a boil. Lower heat and simmer for at least 3 hours.

Vegetable soup is best when prepared a day in advance.

10 servings

Enjoy the hearty goodness of homemade vegetable soup. Linda Wasinger prepares her soup a day in advance allowing the flavors to blend.

Fort Casey is located on the western shore of Central Whidbey. The fort was considered part of the "triangle" defense at the entrance of Puget Sound, with Fort Worden and Fort Flagler on the shores across Admiralty Inlet. The fort was operational during both world wars, however, it was never used in defensive action. Today Fort Casey is a spectacular 137-acre state park. Visitors are welcome to explore the tunnels, picnic, hike on the trails and learn a bit of history while wandering through the turn-of-the-century lighthouse.

Chicken Stock

4 pounds chicken pieces, or 1 whole (4 pound) fryer

2 large onions, chopped in chunks

2 large carrots, chopped in chunks

2 stalks celery, chopped in chunks

6 to 8 fresh parsley sprigs

1/2 teaspoon whole peppercorns

2 teaspoons thyme

2 whole bay leaves

1 teaspoon garlic powder

2 tablespoons worcestershire sauce

1 cup white wine

Trim fat from chicken before placing in a 6-quart stock pot. Add vegetables, all seasonings and wine to the pot with the chicken. Fill the pot with cold water and bring to a boil.

Reduce heat, partially cover pot and allow to simmer on stove for 5 hours. Strain the stock and remove all chicken scraps and bones. Refrigerate overnight. Remove from refrigerator; skim and discard fat.

Store chicken stock in glass jars or tightly covered containers. Refrigerate or freeze and use when needed.

Yield: 8-10 pints

Homemade stocks are well worth the effort and outshine the canned variety. All of the vegetables can be roughly chopped and unpeeled as the stock will be cooked for hours before the vegetables are strained out of the soup. Sid and Bobbie Parker make Beef and Chicken Stock as a joint effort and appreciate having it on hand for use in cooking. Stock may be frozen in ice cube trays and stored in freezer bags.

Beef Stock

5-6 pounds of beef bones
3 tablespoons vegetable oil
1 large celery rib, chopped
2 medium onions, chopped
2 medium carrots, chopped
2 cloves garlic, sliced
1 (14 ounce) can chopped tomatoes
1 cup white wine
1 bay leaf
1/2 teaspoon black peppercorns
1/2 teaspoon worcestershire sauce
1/3 cup fresh parsley, snipped

Preheat oven to 400°.

Place beef bones in a large roasting pan and brown well in the oven for 45 minutes.

Meanwhile, heat oil in a large skillet over medium heat. Add celery, onion, carrots and garlic. Sauté until golden brown. Remove vegetables from skillet with a slotted spoon. Add them to a 6-quart stock pot or kettle.

Add the meat to the stock pot, using a slotted spoon. Add tomatoes, wine, bay leaf, peppercorns, worcestershire sauce and parsley. Drain the meat fat from the roasting pan. Add 1 cup water to the roaster and scrape brown bits of meat from the bottom and edge of the pan. Add this liquid from the roaster to the stock pot with the vegetables.

Fill the stock pot with cold water and bring the soup to a boil. Reduce the heat and simmer beef stock for 6 to 8 hours. Strain the stock and chill. When completely cooled remove fat.

Store beef stock in glass jars or tightly covered containers. Refrigerate or freeze and use when needed.

Yield: 8-10 pints

Beef Stock and Chicken Stock are ingredients found in many recipes. We have capitalized the stocks in all our recipes in this book so that you may refer back to these pages.

Naturally, canned Chicken Broth and Beef Consomme may be substituted for our homemade stocks.

Puget Sound Oyster Bisque

1/4 cup flour
2 teaspoons salt
4 teaspoons worcestershire
3 (10 ounce) jars shucked oysters
6 cups half and half
3 tablespoons margarine
snipped parsley for garnish

In a large saucepan, whisk together flour, 1/4 cup water, salt and worcestershire. Add oysters and their liquid. Depending on the size of the oysters you may want to cut them into bite size pieces. Cook over medium heat for 10 minutes, stirring constantly. The centers will be firm and the edge of oysters will curl a bit when cooked.

Add half and half and margarine and heat to boiling. Let the bisque stand at least 15 minutes to blend flavors.

Garnish with snipped parsley if so desired.

6 servings

The distinctive taste of oysters is a favorite of many Whidbey Island residents. This bisque makes the perfect starter to any entrée. It is equally suitable as a meal in itself when accompanied by a warm loaf of freshly baked bread.

When you are harvesting shellfish on Whidbey Island please don't destroy the land. Remember those rocks you're turning over are someone's home. Replacing turned rocks to their original position guards immature shellfish and enables them to grow. This is also a state law.

Crescent Harbor Clam Chowder

3 cups clams

6 slices bacon

1 large yellow onion, chopped

1 cup diced celery

5 medium potatoes, peeled and diced

1/4 cup butter

1 cup CHICKEN STOCK

6 cups milk

salt and pepper to taste

minced parsley for garnish

Clean and grind, or mince, fresh clams. Place clams in a saucepan and cover them with water. Bring the water to a boil; cook until clams are tender (about 10 minutes). Set aside (without draining).

Dice the bacon in 1-inch pieces. Place the bacon in a small saucepan and cover the bacon with water. Bring to a boil; cook the bacon pieces for 4 minutes. Drain and set aside.

In a large soup kettle, put the onion, celery, and potatoes together and add just enough water to cover them. Simmer the vegetables until they are barely tender (about 10 minutes). Add the butter, stock, milk and seasonings. Add the bacon and the clams with their broth. Simmer the soup for 15 minutes.

Garnish the clam chowder with minced parsley.

10 servings

The earliest recorded inhabitants of Whidbey Island were the Indians. They had a unique method of making clam chowder. After soaking the clams in fresh water overnight, the clams were thrown into a hollowed log containing water heated to boiling by immersion of hot stones. After the clams had opened, they were scraped from their shells and put back into the water. The clams were then soaked with chunks of smoked venison and various roots.

Kay Roodzant shares her recipe for clam chowder with us.

Tutmas Armenian Yogurt Soup

3 3/4 cups CHICKEN STOCK
salt and white pepper to taste
1/3 cup rice
1 tablespoon cornstarch
3 3/4 cups unflavored yogurt
3 egg yolks, lightly beaten
2 1/2 tablespoons butter or olive oil
2 tablespoons dried crushed mint

Season the stock with salt and pepper. Bring to a boil, add the rice and reduce the heat to simmer.

Meanwhile, dissolve the cornstarch in 1/2 cup cold water. In a medium saucepan add the cornstarch to the yogurt and stir well. Add the beaten yolks and stir.

Slowly bring the yogurt mixture to a boil, stirring constantly in one direction. After the mixture has thickened, slowly stir it into the stock and rice. Continue to simmer soup until rice is soft.

In a separate skillet heat butter or oil over low heat and stir in mint. Sauté the mint until soft. Reserve for garnish.

Serve the soup in warm bowls adding a bit of sautéed mint to each individual serving.

6 servings

Café Langley is a difficult restaurant to stroll past. The pungent aroma, friendly service and unpretentious decor hasten our return time after time. This unusual yogurt soup is typical of *Café Langley's* Mediterranean fare.

Mint is an herb that retains its great strength when dried. The best mint for full flavor is spearmint.

Split Pea Soup

2 cups split peas
1/4 cup olive oil
2 carrots, peeled and sliced into rounds
1 clove garlic, minced
1 cup diced yellow onion
1/2 cup chopped celery
1/4 cup fresh minced parsley
2 1/2 teaspoons salt
1/2 teaspoon ground black pepper
1/2 teaspoon basil
1 bay leaf
1 cup milk
2 cups minced ham
Garnish: Parmesan cheese and garlic croutons

Soak the peas for 4 hours in a large bowl of warm water. Drain the water from the peas and rinse. In a large kettle, heat 2 1/2 quarts of water to boiling. Add the peas and allow the water to return to a boil before lowering the heat . Simmer over low heat for 2 1/2 hours while stirring occasionally.

Heat oil in a skillet over medium heat. Add carrots, garlic, onion and celery and sauté for 10 minutes. Add the vegetable mixture and all seasonings to peas and continue to simmer over low heat for another 30 minutes.

Remove and discard the bay leaf. Purée the soup 2 minutes in an electric blender. Add the ham and blend for 1 minute more. It may be necessary to blend portions of the soup at a time.

The soup may be refrigerated and reheated the following day. If the soup seems too thick, add a bit of CHICKEN STOCK and blend. Garnish as suggested.

8 servings

We asked some pea soup connoisseurs to test this recipe. Adults and kids alike gave it "two thumbs up."

This Split Pea soup is excellent garnished with Parmesan cheese and garlic croutons.

Squash Soup

3 cups cooked squash
1 cup chopped onion
2 tablespoons butter
1 tablespoon flour
3 cups CHICKEN STOCK
1/2 teaspoon salt
freshly ground pepper to taste
1/2 cup heavy cream, whipped

Garnish: nutmeg
    3 tablespoons squash seeds, toasted

Purée cooked squash in an electric blender. In a large heavy saucepan over low heat, sauté the onion in butter until it turns soft. Sprinkle in flour and cook, stirring constantly for 2 to 3 minutes.

Gradually add stock, whisking thoroughly. Add squash purée and simmer gently for 15 minutes. Stir in salt and pepper.

Pour the heated soup into warm bowls and top each with a dollop of whipped cream, sprinkle of nutmeg and some toasted squash seeds.

6 *servings*

This soup is a preferred recipe from the Sherman squash farm.

Cashew Mushroom Soup

2 tablespoons butter or margarine
2 tablespoons flour
1 1/2 cups CHICKEN STOCK
1 1/3 cups half and half
dash ground nutmeg
salt and pepper to taste
2 cups sliced fresh mushrooms
1 cup cashews, coarsely chopped

Garnish: whole cashews and sliced mushrooms

In a 2-quart saucepan, melt the butter or margarine. Stir in the flour. Add chicken stock, half and half, nutmeg, salt and pepper. Cook and stir over medium heat until mixture has thickened. Stir in the mushrooms and half of the cashews and cook, while stirring, for 2 more minutes. Pour half of the soup mixture into a blender or food processor and process until fairly smooth. Do the same with the other half of the soup mixture.

Return all to saucepan and stir in remaining chopped nuts. Season to taste and heat through.

Garnish individual servings with whole cashews and sliced mushrooms.

6 servings

This variation of a favorite soup combines intriguing textures and flavors.

Cream of Broccoli Soup

1 bunch of broccoli (about 1 1/2 pounds)
1/4 cup butter
2 yellow onions
2 cups chopped celery
1 clove garlic, minced
1/2 cup flour
4 cups milk
4 cups CHICKEN STOCK
1/2 teaspoon thyme
1/2 teaspoon marjoram
salt and pepper to taste

Garnish: sliced almonds and chopped tomato

Wash and trim broccoli; cut into 1/2 inch pieces. Steam in salted water until tender. Drain and set aside.

In a large saucepan, melt the butter and sauté onions, celery and garlic. Stir in flour, milk, chicken stock, and herbs. Stir over low heat until soup thickens and boils.

In a food processor or blender, finely chop at least half of the broccoli. Add all of the broccoli, salt and pepper to the soup.

Gently reheat soup at serving time. Garnish individual servings with sliced almonds and chopped tomato.

8 servings

A warm, homemade soup is good for both body and soul. In fact, nothing makes a more heartfelt gift for a friend or neighbor than a pot of soup prepared in your own kitchen.

Garnish the top of this soup with sliced almonds and chopped tomato.

"It breathes reassurance, it offers consolation; after a weary day it promotes sociability … There is nothing like a bowl of hot soup."

– Louis DeGouy

Golden Onion Soup

6 tablespoons butter

4 medium onions, thinly sliced

1 tablespoon sugar

2 teaspoons flour

1 teaspoon dry mustard

1/2 teaspoon curry

2 cloves garlic, minced

1 bay leaf

·2 teaspoons worcestershire sauce

1 cup white wine

4 cups CHICKEN STOCK

4 slices French bread

2 cups grated Swiss, Romano or Provolone cheese
   or a combination of all three

Melt butter in a heavy skillet and add onions. Sauté the onions over medium heat for 30 minutes, stirring often until onions are golden brown.

Add sugar, flour, mustard and curry to onions. Stir for 1 minute until blended. Add garlic, bay leaf, worcestershire sauce, wine and stock. Mix well and bring to a boil over medium high heat. Reduce to low heat and simmer for 25 minutes. Remove the bay leaf.

Toast bread slices under broiler, turning once. Reduce temperature to 250° and dry toast for 20 minutes.

Ladle soup into ovenproof bowls on a baking sheet and top with toasted French bread slices. Sprinkle with cheese and broil 4 inches from heat until cheese has melted.

Serve immediately with a Caesar Salad and fresh baguettes.

8 servings

To pamper his wife on a cozy evening at home, Sid Parker prepares Golden Onion Soup. The mellow flavor is derived from the combination of white wine, chicken stock and curry.

Throughout the centuries onions have been thought to have medicinal powers, such as the prevention of dysentery, and improvement in eyesight. In fact, at the height of the Civil War, General Grant fired off an urgent message to the War Department saying, "I will not move my Army without onions!"

Chilled Vegetable Soup

1 cup diced, raw potatoes
1 cup fresh or frozen peas
1/4 cup sliced green onion
1 1/2 cups CHICKEN STOCK
1/8 teaspoon celery salt
1/4 teaspoon curry powder
1 cup heavy cream or half and half

In a large saucepan cook the vegetables in the stock over medium heat until tender. Pour the vegetables and stock into a blender or food processor, and blend until smooth.

Add the celery salt, curry powder and cream to the stock; mix well.

Chill the soup in the refrigerator. Serve cold.

4 servings

Lois and Dwight Mitchell enjoy this soup while they are aboard their boat cruising the San Juan Islands.

"A *hot soup must be steaming; a cold soup must be chilled as thoroughly and carefully as we would a fine champagne.*"

– Charles H. Baker, Jr.

Vichyssoise

1 bunch green onions
1 yellow onion
1/4 cup butter
4 cups CHICKEN STOCK
3 large potatoes, peeled and thinly sliced
1 cup heavy cream
1 cup half and half
salt and pepper to taste
chopped green onion tops for garnish

Finely chop the white parts of the green onions. Save the green onion tops for garnish. Thinly slice the yellow onion and cook it with the green onions in butter until they are fork tender. Stir in the stock and sliced potatoes. Cover, and cook over low heat for 30 minutes.

Pour the soup into an electric blender and blend until smooth. Pour in heavy cream and half and half. Season with salt and pepper. Chill for several hours in the refrigerator.

Serve the soup well chilled with green onion tops for garnish.

8 servings

When the summer temperature soars prepare Vichyssoise early in the day. This cold potato soup served with fresh fruit and a green salad makes an easy and refreshing warm weather meal.

Our research reveals that "Vichyssoise" was created by a chef at the Ritz-Carlton Hotel in New York City in 1910.

Saratoga Summer Salad

1/2 sweet red onion
1 fresh orange, peeled
1 cucumber, peeled
1 head romaine lettuce
1 ripe avocado, peeled and sliced

Sun Kissed Dressing

Slice sweet onion, orange and cucumber into thin rings. Tear romaine into bite size pieces. Toss in a large salad bowl and add sliced avocado. Pour dressing over all.

On a warm "Indian summer" evening, nothing will enhance your barbeque more than Saratoga Summer Salad. Make the "Sun Kissed" dressing several hours in advance to take full advantage of this appealing combination of citrus flavors.

Sun Kissed Dressing

1/2 teaspoon grated lemon peel
1/2 teaspoon grated orange peel
1/3 cup orange juice concentrate
1 1/2 tablespoons sugar
1/2 cup vegetable oil
2 tablespoons red wine vinegar
1 tablespoon fresh lemon juice
1/4 teaspoon salt
pepper to taste

Spin the above ingredients in an electric blender to mix well. Store in a container with a tight-fitting lid.

6 servings

Ebey's Landing is one of a few protected historical sites and cultural landscapes accorded national significance in the National Parks and Recreation Act of 1978. The purpose of the reserve is "to preserve and protect a rural community which provides an unbroken historic record from the nineteenth century exploration and settlement of Puget Sound to the present time," according to the legislation that established it.

Ebey's Landing Historical Reserve encompasses 22 square miles of historic and scenic terrain including 91 nationally registered historic structures.

Green Salad with Purple Chive Flowers

6-8 slices bacon
1 dozen chive flowers
1/2 head iceburg lettuce
1/2 pound broccoli

1/4 pound mushrooms, sliced
1/2 red onion, thinly sliced
    into rings

Boiled Dressing

Fry bacon, drain and cool. Break into bits.

Pick chive flowers from stems. Rinse lightly and drain well. Set aside.

Tear lettuce into bite size pieces and place in a large bowl. Remove broccoli flowerettes from stem and add to lettuce. Add mushrooms and onions to lettuce. Toss bacon bits and chive flowers into salad; chill until serving.

This imaginative salad was created to utilize the purple chive blooms that appear each spring. Serve the salad in a crystal bowl to spotlight the vigorous spring colors.

Boiled Dressing

1 whole egg
1 egg yolk
1/2 cup sugar
1/2 teaspoon dry mustard
1 1/2 teaspoon cornstarch

1/2 cup vinegar
pinch of salt
2 tablespoons butter
1/2 cup mayonnaise

Beat together the whole egg and yolk. Stir in sugar, mustard, cornstarch, and 1/4 cup vinegar.

In a small saucepan combine 1/4 cup water, salt and 1/4 cup vinegar. Bring to a boil. Reduce heat and add egg mixture. Continue to cook, stirring constantly until thick. Remove from heat.

Stir butter and mayonnaise into dressing.

Chill in an airtight container. This may be stored for several days in the refrigerator.

8 servings

Artichoke Caesar Salad

1 (6 ounce) jar marinated artichoke hearts,
    reserve marinade
1 head romaine lettuce
1/4 cup freshly grated Parmesan cheese
1 cup toasted sourdough bread croutons

Caesar Dressing

Drain marinade from artichokes. Reserve for dressing.

Tear lettuce into bite size pieces and put in a salad bowl. Cut artichoke hearts into small pieces and add to lettuce. Sprinkle salad with Parmesan and croutons. Pour Caesar Dressing over salad; toss to coat.

Caesar Dressing

marinade from artichoke hearts
1/4 cup olive oil
2 tablespoons lemon juice
1 raw egg yolk
1/2 teaspoon Dijon mustard
1/4 teaspoon garlic salt
1/4 cup grated Parmesan cheese

Combine all ingredients and add to salad just before serving.

4 servings

Our version of the classic Caesar salad is easy to assemble and a welcome addition to an elegant meal.

In 1985 the U.S. Supreme Court handed down a verdict which gave Whidbey Island the distinction of being the longest island in the continental United States.

Whidbey Island is 45 miles long and 210 square miles.

Cherita's Orange Mushroom Salad

1 teaspoon margarine

1/4 cup sliced almonds

4 slices bacon

2 large heads butter lettuce

1 can mandarin oranges, drained

1/2 pound fresh mushrooms, sliced

1/2 pound cooked shrimp, optional

Blue Cheese Dressing

Melt the margarine in a small skillet and cook almonds until brown. Set aside. Cook bacon until crisp; drain and crumble. Tear lettuce into bite size pieces and place in a salad bowl. Add oranges. Toss mushrooms, bacon, almonds and shrimp into the salad.

Enjoy the flavors of orange, blue cheese and bacon in this impressive salad sent to us by Cherita Koetje.

Blue Cheese Dressing

6 tablespoons salad oil

3 tablespoons white wine vinegar

3 tablespoons crumbled blue cheese

1/4 teaspoon each salt and dry mustard

pepper to taste

In a small bowl mix together the oil, vinegar, cheese, salt, pepper and mustard. Chill.

When ready to serve the salad, pour the dressing over the salad and toss lightly.

8 servings

Whidbey Spinach Salad

1 large bunch fresh spinach

3 kiwi

1 cup fresh pineapple, cut into 1-inch chunks

Poppyseed Dressing or Orange Creamed Dressing

Tear spinach into bite size pieces. Peel and slice kiwi and add to spinach. Combine pineapple with greens. Just before serving, pour dressing over salad to coat.

This salad is a particular favorite because you can easily substitute the fresh fruit according to season and availability. We've used fresh strawberries, mandarin oranges and grapefruit.

Poppyseed Dressing

1/4 cup sugar

1 tablespoon sesame seeds

1 tablespoon poppyseeds

1 1/2 tablespoons diced onion flakes

1/4 teaspoon worcestershire sauce

1/2 cup vegetable oil

1/4 cup red vinegar

In a small bowl combine all ingredients and whisk until well blended. Dressing may be stored in an airtight container in the refrigerator.

Orange Creamed Dressing

1 cup heavy cream, whipped

2 tablespoons orange flavored liqueur

1/2 cup chopped green onion

Fold all ingredients together and refrigerate until serving.

4 servings

Vegetables in Mint Marinade

3 medium tomatoes
1 green or red pepper
4 green onions
1 cucumber, peeled
12 radishes
1/2 cup chopped parsley

Mint Marinade

We like to serve this colorful, crunchy salad on a bed of romaine.

Coarsely chop vegetables to uniform size. Place in a large bowl. Pour Mint Marinade over all and refrigerate several hours before serving.

Mint Marinade

1 tablespoon mint, chopped
1 clove garlic, minced
1/4 cup olive oil
juice of 2 lemons
salt and pepper to taste
1/2 cup feta cheese, crumbled

Combine all ingredients, except cheese, and pour over vegetables. Mix to coat and allow to marinate for one hour prior to serving.

Crumble feta cheese over the top of the vegetables when ready to serve.

8 servings

Sweet red peppers are more perishable than green peppers. Keep sweet peppers, unwashed, in the crisper drawer of the refrigerator. Use within a week before they begin to lose moisture and shrivel.

Shanghai Chicken Salad

1 whole chicken breast
Marinade: 2 teaspoons soy sauce
              2 teaspoons sesame oil
              1/2 teaspoon salt
              1/4 teaspoon pepper
1/2 head iceberg lettuce
1/2 cup chopped green onions
1 cup fresh pea pods
1/2 cup chopped celery
1 ounce rice sticks
1/4 cup oil
1/4 cup slivered almonds for garnish
1/2 tablespoon sesame seeds for garnish

Dressing

Textures characteristic of Asian cuisine combine to make this main course salad healthful and tasty.

Bone, skin and cut the chicken into thin strips. Combine soy sauce, sesame oil, salt and pepper in a medium size bowl. Add chicken and marinate for 30 minutes while preparing salad.

Tear lettuce into bite size pieces and place in a large salad bowl. Add green onions, pea pods, celery and refrigerate.

In a wok or large frying pan heat oil over high heat. Break rice sticks into 1-inch pieces as they are dropped into the wok, a handful at a time. As soon as the rice sticks reach the hot oil they will puff up and should be removed immediately from the heat with slotted spoon. Drain on a paper towel.

Add chicken to remaining oil and stir fry for 4 minutes. Drain chicken on paper towels and allow to cool. Add cooled chicken to salad greens.

Pour dressing over all and toss. Garnish with slivered almonds and sesame seeds. Top with rice sticks.

Continued on next page

Shanghai Chicken Salad continued

Dressing

2 teaspoons sugar
1/4 cup oil
1/4 cup rice vinegar

1/4 cup soy sauce
1/2 teaspoon salt
2 teaspoons sesame oil

Combine all ingredients and blend well.

4 servings

Tarragon Asparagus

1 1/2 pounds asparagus, tough ends removed

In a large frying pan with 1/2 inch boiling water, cook asparagus over medium high heat until tender (about 7 minutes). Drain; plunge into ice water. When asparagus is cool, remove from water and drain. Place asparagus in a chilled serving dish. Prepare vinaigrette.

Vinaigrette

1/4 cup white wine vinegar
1/4 cup olive oil or vegetable oil
1 tablespoon fresh or 1 teaspoon dry tarragon

Combine ingredients and pour the vinaigrette over the stalks. Turn the asparagus to coat evenly.

6 servings

Highlight the taste of springtime asparagus with this vegetable vinaigrette. Tarragon Asparagus works beautifully as a dish that can be prepared a day ahead of serving when covered and chilled. A refreshing vegetable that complements any meal.

Curried Chicken Luncheon Salad

4 whole chicken breasts, cooked

1 (8 ounce) can sliced water chestnuts

1 pound green seedless grapes

1 cup sliced celery

1 1/2 cups toasted slivered almonds

1 1/2 teaspoons curry powder

1 1/2 teaspoons soy sauce

1 1/2 cups mayonnaise

1 (8 ounce) can pineapple tidbits, drained or 1 cup fresh pineapple pieces

sliced almonds for garnish

Coarsely cut the chicken meat from the bone into bite size pieces. In a large bowl combine the chicken with water chestnuts, grapes, celery and almonds. Set aside.

In a small bowl blend the curry powder and soy sauce into the mayonnaise. Fold the curry mixture into the bowl of chicken and mix well. Chill for several hours or cover and refrigerate overnight.

When ready to serve the salad, add the pineapple to the chicken mixture. If desired, use additional almonds as garnish.

6 servings

Let this enticing salad star as the centerpiece on your luncheon table. Present the salad on a platter lined with lettuce or spinach leaves. In the summer time add violet colored "Johnny Jump Up" flower blooms to your display to entice your guests further. The blooms are edible, of course!

Curried Chicken Salad is also wonderful when served in the middle of freshly baked croissants.

Northwest Seafood Salad

Sesame Dressing

2 dozen large shrimp, shelled and deveined
1 1/2 pound scallops
1/2 pound snow peas
2 cucumbers, peeled and sliced
4 celery stalks, sliced

Prepare Sesame Dressing.

Cook shrimp in boiling water for 2 minutes or until they are pink. Drain well and transfer to a small bowl. Cool slightly. When they are cool, spoon 3 tablespoons dressing over shrimp and refrigerate until serving.

Cook scallops in boiling water until white and opaque. Drain well and chill. Place snow peas in a colander and pour boiling water over them. Drain well. Transfer snow peas to a salad bowl and add cucumbers and celery. Toss slightly and chill.

To assemble, add scallops and shrimp to the salad bowl. Pour dressing over all and toss to coat.

Sesame Dressing

1/3 cup white vinegar
1/4 cup vegetable oil
3 tablespoons soy sauce
2 tablespoons dry mustard
2 tablespoons sesame oil
2 tablespoons sherry
1 tablespoon sugar

Combine all ingredients in a jar with 1/3 cup water. Shake well to mix.

4 servings

Garnish each serving of this colorful main dish salad with a lemon quarter. Let it be the focus of a summer party.

Dilled Shrimp Salad

2 heads butter lettuce
3 ounces Monterey Jack cheese
1 cucumber
1/2 pound small shrimp

Dill Dressing

Tear butter lettuce into bite size pieces and place in a large
salad bowl. Cut jack cheese into 1/4 inch cubes and spread
over lettuce. Peel and slice cucumbers 1/2 inch thick and add
to salad. Rinse and drain shrimp before adding to the salad.

Pour dressing over all, toss and serve.

The zest of the dill and bite
size pieces of Jack cheese create
a surprising enhancement to the
shrimp. We grow nasturtiums
in our gardens because they
flourish in abundance and are
used nicely as a delicate garnish.
A bloom or two placed on
individual servings of this salad
enhances the bright color of the
shrimp.

Dill Dressing

1/4 cup olive oil
1 1/2 tablespoons white wine vinegar
1 tablespoon fresh lemon juice
1/2 teaspoon dill weed
1/4 teaspoon salt
1/8 teaspoon dry mustard
dash of pepper
1 clove garlic, minced

Combine all dressing ingredients and blend well. Allow
dressing to marinate for one hour before using on the salad.

6 servings

*Nasturtiums grown in
your garden will deter pests
and encourage growth of other
vegetables. Other edible flowers
include: Gladiolus, Forget-Me-
Not, Violet, Day Lily, Johnny-
Jump-Up, Roses, Lavender and
Honeysuckle. Make sure all
blooms are pesticide-free before
using them with your food.*

Smoked Salmon Rice Salad

1 cup long grain rice
1 cup wild rice
1 zucchini, shredded
1 carrot, shredded
4 green onions, chopped
2 tablespoons chopped
    parsley
1 tablespoon lemon juice
1/4 cup balsamic vinegar

2 cloves garlic, minced
1/3 cup olive oil
1/2 pound smoked
    salmon
salt and pepper to taste
1 tablespoon sliced olives
    for garnish
1 tablespoon chopped
    pecans for garnish

Cook long grain and wild rice according to package directions. Allow to cool. Place shredded zucchini and carrot in salad bowl. Add cooled rice, green onions and parsley. Mix well.

In a small bowl whisk together lemon juice, balsamic vinegar and minced garlic. Slowly whisk in olive oil. Add salt and pepper to taste.

To serve, toss salad mixture with dressing. Crumble salmon on top and garnish with sliced olives and chopped pecans.

8 servings

Within a short walk of Coupeville's harbor dock *Christopher's Restaurant* offers intimate dining with a personal touch. We are pleased to give you the recipe for one of Christopher Panek's delicious creations.

Smoked Salmon Niçoise

On individual lettuce lined salad plates, arrange slices of smoked salmon, several cooked green beans, red onion slices, black olives, anchovy filets (if desired), several cherry tomatoes and slices of hard boiled eggs. Serve with a garlic vinaigrette dressing.

Try Jim Seabolt's method of preparing a smoked salmon salad.

Oriental Smoked Salmon

On individual serving plates, arrange thin slices of smoked salmon in spoke-like fashion. Mound grated white radish and 1/4 teaspoon grated fresh ginger in the center. Using a fresh lime, squeeze juice over salmon and sprinkle with finely chopped parsley. Serve with soy sauce.

Avocado Ring with Honeycream Dressing

1 (6 ounce) package lime jello
1/4 teaspoon salt
2 ripe avocados, peeled
2 tablespoons lemon juice

Honeycream Dressing

Dissolve jello and salt in 2 cups boiling water. Chill until slightly thickened. Mash avocados with lemon juice. Use a wire whisk to blend the avocado with the jello. Pour into a jello ring or mold. Chill until firm.

Honeycream Dressing

1/2 cup mayonnaise
1 tablespoon honey
1/2 cup sliced strawberries

Blend ingredients and serve as an accompaniment to the molded salad.

8 servings

Prepare a colorful and mouth watering smoked salmon salad. It will certainly leave your guests yearning for more. Compliments of *Seabolt's Smokehouse*.

Joyce DeJong serves this appealing salad molded in a ring. The dressing is spooned from a small dish in the center of the ring. Fresh strawberries surround the salad as a delightful garnish.

Try to find bumpy, thick skinned avocados for fullest flavor.

Holiday Salad

2 1/2 cups coarsely crushed pretzels
3/4 cup butter, melted
3 teaspoons powdered sugar

Preheat oven to 325°.

Mix pretzels, butter and sugar; spread in a 9 x 13 inch pan.

Bake at 325° for 10 minutes. Allow to cool.

1 (8 ounce) package cream cheese, softened
1 cup powdered sugar
1 (8 ounce) container Cool Whip

In a bowl, beat the cream cheese and powdered sugar together.
Fold in Cool Whip. Chill.

1 teaspoon lemon juice
1 (6 ounce) package raspberry jello
2 (8 ounce) packages frozen raspberries

Combine lemon juice and 2 cups boiling water. Stir in the
jello to dissolve. Add raspberries. Let the mixture gel at room
temperature until thickened, but not entirely set. Spread over
the cream cheese.

Refrigerate the salad until gelatin has set.

12 servings

This festive layered salad
can be made ahead and will
travel well to your annual
holiday buffet. Your family and
friends will have fun guessing
the contents of the base.

*"Come in the evening, come
in the morning, Come when
expected, come without warning;
Thousands of welcomes you'll
find here before you, And the
oftener you come, the more we'll
adore you."*

Irish Rhyme

Spaghetti Salad

1 pound spaghetti; cooked, drained and rinsed
1/2 cup chopped green onion
1/2 cup diced red or green pepper
1 medium zucchini, sliced
12 cherry tomatoes, quartered
1 (4 ounce) can sliced black olives, drained
1 (6 ounce) jar marinated artichoke hearts, halved

Italian Dressing

Combine all ingredients. Add dressing, season to taste and toss.

A welcome advantage of this flavorful and unusual salad is that a well stocked pantry will contain the ingredients needed. We think this is the perfect picnic fare.

Italian Dressing

1 (8 ounce) bottle Italian dressing
1/2 cup red wine vinegar
1 teaspoon salt
1/4 teaspoon pepper
2 tablespoons salad seasoning (such as "Johnny's Salad Elegance")
1/2 cup grated Parmesan cheese

Combine all ingredients together and mix well.

12 servings

This salad will stay fresh for up to 1 week when refrigerated. Add other vegetables as desired and a bit more dressing to the salad before serving.

Peg's Pasta Salad

1/2 pound rotini pasta
1/2 pound broccoli
1/2 head romaine lettuce
4 green onions, chopped
12 black Greek olives
1 tomato, diced
1 cup crumbled feta cheese

Vinegar and Oil Dressing

Peggy Moore created this pasta salad, enriched with vegetables, to serve at a luncheon on her deck overlooking Penn Cove. Because this salad is made ahead of serving she could relax and enjoy the afternoon.

Cook pasta according to package directions.

Remove stems from broccoli and cut flowerettes into bite size pieces. Blanche in boiling water for 2 minutes. Remove from boiling water and plunge broccoli into a large bowl of ice water. Drain broccoli.

Tear romaine leaves into bite size pieces. Place in a large salad bowl. Add broccoli, cooked pasta, green onions, olives and diced tomato.

Just before serving pour dressing over all and sprinkle with cheese.

The Coupeville Arts and Crafts Festival was started in 1964 to raise money for restoring historic buildings on Front Street. The festival association also parented the Coupeville Arts Center. The Center provides an assortment of arts workshops throughout the year.

Vinegar and Oil Dressing

1/3 cup vinegar
2/3 cup olive oil
1 teaspoon salt
1 teaspoon pepper
1 teaspoon dry mustard
2 cloves garlic, minced

Combine ingredients in a jar with a tight fitting lid and shake to mix.

8 servings

Green Salad Dressings

Dijon Vinaigrette

1 teaspoon Dijon mustard
2 tablespoons red wine vinegar
1/2 teaspoon salt
1/4 teaspoon black pepper

pinch of fresh or dried
  tarragon
2 cloves garlic, minced
1/4 cup olive oil

Combine all ingredients. Cover and chill. Blend before
serving.

Yield: 1/2 cup

Store all salad dressings in
tightly covered containers in
the refrigerator and use within
2 weeks.

Roquefort Dressing

4 ounces roquefort cheese
1/4 cup olive oil
5 drops tabasco

1 clove garlic, minced
juice of a fresh lemon
1 egg, slightly beaten

Crumble cheese in a small bowl. Pour olive oil over cheese.
Add tabasco, garlic, lemon juice and egg. Mix together and
refrigerate until serving.

Yield: 1/2 cup

Marie's Onion Dressing

1 small onion
1/3 cup catsup
1/2 cup salad oil
1/4 cup wine vinegar

1/3 cup sugar
1 teaspoon salt
1 tablespoon worcestershire
1 1/2 teaspoons paprika

Finely grate onion into a small bowl. Add the other dressing
ingredients and mix well. Refrigerate and blend before serving.

Yield: 1 1/2 cups

Mustard Sour Cream Dressing

1/4 cup sour cream
1/4 cup Dijon mustard
1 egg
3/4 cup salad oil

1/4 cup red wine vinegar
1/2 teaspoon minced garlic
dash worcestershire sauce
pinch salt and white pepper

Mix sour cream and mustard together in a food processor or electric blender. Add egg and blend slowly. While machine continues to run, pour in oil followed by vinegar. Add garlic, worcestershire, salt and pepper.

Yield: 1 1/2 cups

The *Captain Whidbey Inn* house dressing.

B's Pineapple Dressing

juice from 1 (20 ounce) can pineapple chunks
3/4 cup sugar
2 tablespoons flour
2 eggs, separated
3 tablespoons butter
1/2 cup whipped cream

Drain juice from pineapple. Reserve pineapple for use in the salad. Heat juice in a saucepan over medium heat. Blend together sugar and flour; add to juice. Slightly beat egg yolks and add to the heated mixture.

Beat egg whites until stiff. Remove juice mixture from heat. Fold in egg whites and butter. Cool. Fold in whipped cream just before serving the dressing over individual servings of fruit.

Yield: 2 cups

Bea Peterson's Bed and Breakfast (B's B&B) is perched on a hill with a sweeping view of Clinton's lush farmland. Watch the ferries motor between Clinton and Mukilteo from your own private deck surrounded by a rolling lawn and fruit trees.

"August for the people and their favourite islands. Daily the steamers sidle up to meet the effusive welcome of the pier."

– W.H. Auden

Fruit Salad Dressings

Sweet Wine Dressing

3 egg yolks   1/3 cup sweet white wine
1/3 cup sugar

In a small saucepan mix all ingredients over medium heat until thickened. Stir briskly. Store in the refrigerator.

Yield: 2/3 cup

Curry Dressing

2/3 cup plain yogurt   1 teaspoon fresh lime juice
1 tablespoon honey   1/4 teaspoon curry powder

Combine all ingredients; stir well. Refrigerate.

Yield: 2/3 cup

Honey Dressing

1 cup vegetable oil   1 tablespoon dry mustard
1/4 cup vinegar   1 tablespoon celery seed
1/2 cup honey

Mix the ingredients together until thoroughly blended. Refrigerate.

Yield: 1 1/2 cups

Ginger Lime Dressing

1/2 cup mayonnaise   1 tablespoon lime juice
1/2 cup sour cream   1 tablespoon honey
2 teaspoons grated lime peel   1/2 teaspoon ginger

Combine all ingredients until blended. Refrigerate.

Yield: 1 cup

Add a bit of pizazz to a fresh fruit salad, or melon slices, with any of these refreshing dressings.

Ebey's Landing Squash Farms
Coupeville

Island County Fair

It wouldn't be summer on Whidbey Island without the Island County Fair. The four-day affair in August features a logging show, 4-H competition and demonstrations, a calf scramble, games and nostalgic entertainment.

Fiesta Bean Dip with Tortilla Chips

Stuffed Burgers

Fruit Salad with Ginger Lime Dressing

Potatoes with Rosemary and Garlic

Fresh Raspberry Pie

Choochokum Festival of the Arts, Langley

Choochokum, Langley's Festival of the Arts, is a colorful arts and crafts fair featuring top drawer artists and artisans as well as exotic food, music and entertainment. Choochokum is held on the Fourth of July weekend.

Crab Deviled Eggs

Raspberry Lemonade Drink

Curried Chicken Luncheon Salad

Sliced Tomatoes with Pesto Vinaigrette

Yeast Rolls

Bell's Strawberry Tart

Squash Fluff

3 1/2 cups cooked squash
1 (8 ounce) can crushed pineapple
1/2 cup sliced water chestnuts
1/2 cup brown sugar
1/2 teaspoon salt
1 tablespoon cream sherry
3 tablespoons butter, melted
1/2 cup fine dry bread crumbs

Preheat oven to 350°.

With a fork blend squash, pineapple, water chestnuts, brown sugar, salt, sherry, and 2 tablespoons butter. Turn into a shallow 1-quart greased baking dish.

Stir remaining 1 tablespoon butter into bread crumbs and spread evenly over squash.

Bake at 350° for 40 minutes and serve warm.

8 servings

One of the most magnificent sights on the whole island is the view of the lush, fertile farmland outside Coupeville called Ebey's Landing. Some of the earliest Whidbey settlers arrived near this place and were rewarded with riches in produce; the result of their hard work.

Our friends, Ed and Jean Sherman, are sharing some of their favorite recipes utilizing the ever abundant hubbard squash.

Ebey's Landing has been cultivated since at least the mid-19th century. The rich, dark soil has produced Camas for the Indians, wheat, potatoes, squash, pumpkins, alfalfa, and green vegetables. It is also home for two of the largest dairy farms in Western Washington.

Ebey's Prairie has great historical significance and played a large part in early Whidbey Island settlement by Colonel Ebey and others. Ebey's Landing is now a National Reserve.

Year-round Zucchini

6 slices bacon, reserve grease
3 medium zucchini, cut into 1/4-inch slices
3 tomatoes, coarsely chopped
1/2 cup grated sharp cheddar cheese

Fry bacon in a skillet until crisp. Remove bacon to cool. Sauté zucchini slices in bacon grease for 5 minutes. Do not overcook. Add tomatoes and continue cooking 2-3 minutes. Crumble bacon into skillet and cover with grated cheese.

Remove vegetables to a serving dish.

6 servings

In the middle of a long island winter take yourself back to the sunny carefree days of summer. Jane O'Kelley sautés this year-round vegetable with pleasant accents of tomato, cheese and bacon.

Zucchini Gruyère

2 eggs
1 cup heavy cream
1/4 cup plus 1 tablespoon Gruyère cheese, grated
salt and pepper to taste
1 1/4 pounds zucchini

Preheat oven to 400°.

In a small bowl whisk together eggs and cream. Add 1/4 cup cheese and salt and pepper to taste.

Cut zucchini into 1/4-inch slices. Bring 1/2 cup water to a boil in a small saucepan. Add zucchini, cover, and cook 5 minutes or until zucchini is tender. Transfer zucchini to an ovenproof dish.

Pour cream mixture over zucchini. Sprinkle with remaining tablespoon grated cheese. Bake for 10 minutes and serve immediately.

6 servings

When your garden is bursting with fresh zucchini try this as an alternative to your steamed and sautéed methods of preparation.

Glazed Carrots

1 pound carrots
4 tablespoons butter
salt and pepper to taste

2 tablespoons dry sherry
minced parsley

A Simply Whidbey favorite ...

Peel carrots; cut into julienne strips. Cook carrots in a steamer basket until tender (about 4 minutes).

Melt butter in a skillet over medium heat. When the butter begins to brown, add the carrots, salt and pepper. Completely coat the carrots with the butter. Remove carrots to a warm serving dish.

Stir sherry into the butter in the skillet and pour over carrots. Sprinkle the carrots with minced parsley and serve.

4 servings

Autumn Baked Carrots

4 large carrots, peeled and sliced
2 medium apples, peeled and sliced
1/4 cup raisins
2 tablespoons butter, melted
1 tablespoon sugar
1/2 teaspoon cinnamon

Welcome the brisk return of fall with this hearty combination of vegetable and fruit. Paired with a succulent pork roast this will be a near perfect meal.

Do not store carrots near apples. Apples exude an ethylene gas as they ripen which makes the carrots taste bitter.

Preheat oven to 350°.

Cook carrots in boiling water until tender; set aside.

Combine apples and 1/2 cup cold water in saucepan. Cover pan and cook over medium low heat until just tender. Add raisins and cook for 2 or 3 minutes more. Remove from heat and drain well.

Combine all ingredients in a large bowl and add butter, sugar and cinnamon. Stir to coat. Pour into a 1-quart casserole and bake at 350° for 15 minutes.

4 servings

Brussels Sprouts and Onions in Savory Wine Sauce

2 pounds small white boiling onions

1 pound Brussels sprouts

1/4 cup butter

1/4 cup flour

1 cup half and half

1/2 cup Sauterne wine

2 tablespoons minced parsley

3 tablespoons chopped almonds

salt and pepper to taste

paprika for garnish

Peel onions and cook uncovered in a generous amount of salted water for 20 to 25 minutes or until tender. Drain onions, reserving 1/2 cup liquid. Set onions and liquid aside.

Blanche Brussels sprouts in 1 quart boiling salted water for 5 minutes. Drain well.

Melt butter in a medium saucepan. Stir in flour until well blended. Add half and half, Sauterne and liquid from onions. Cook, stirring constantly, until mixture has thickened. Add parsley, almonds, salt and pepper.

Preheat oven to 400°.

Combine sauce and vegetables. Turn into a greased casserole. Sprinkle paprika over the casserole.

Bake at 400° for 25 minutes. The casserole should be golden brown and bubbly.

6 servings

Peggy Moore suggests serving this unusual and flavorful vegetable dish with turkey.

Brussels sprouts can also be boiled, drained and puréed. Stir in bits of butter, a tablespoon of lemon juice and 1/4 cup half and half. Reheat to serve warm. Garnish with bits of bacon.

Swiss Onion Bake

7 1/2 cups chopped sweet onions
4 tablespoons butter
1/2 cup long grain rice
3/4 cup grated Swiss cheese
2/3 cup half and half

Preheat oven to 300°.

In a large skillet, melt butter and sauté onions over medium heat.

Cook rice in 5 cups boiling salted water for 5 minutes. Drain and mix the rice with the onions. Add cheese and half and half.

Bake at 300° in a covered casserole for 1 hour. Allow to set for 10 minutes before serving.

8 servings

Tina Salter prepares this recipe for Swiss Onion Bake each time her family barbeques salmon. She claims it is a natural accompaniment to the classic Northwest meal.

We recommend using Walla Walla sweet onions.

Herbed Spinach

2 (12 ounce) packages frozen chopped spinach, thawed
3 cups cooked rice
2 cups grated sharp cheddar cheese
4 eggs, slightly beaten
4 tablespoons butter, melted

Preheat oven to 350°.

Squeeze spinach to remove moisture. Combine all ingredients and stir until blended. Pour into a buttered 2-quart casserole.

Bake at 350° for 30 minutes or until knife inserted in center comes out clean.

Serve immediately.

8-10 servings

Round out a winter meal for a family gathering with this easy-to-assemble vegetable casserole.

Spinach Stuffed Tomatoes

8 large, firm tomatoes

1 tablespoon butter

1 medium onion, finely chopped

3/4 pound fresh spinach or 1 (10 ounce) package
   frozen chopped spinach, thawed

1 1/4 cups grated Parmesan cheese

2 tablespoons fine, dry bread crumbs

1/8 teaspoon nutmeg

Rinse and dry tomatoes. Cut off the top quarter of each tomato
and discard tops. Using a small spoon, scoop the pulp out of
each tomato, reserving the pulp. The tomatoes should form
sturdy hollow shells for filling. Set shells aside. Chop the pulp
and allow to drain well.

Rinse and drain spinach thoroughly. If you are using frozen
spinach, squeeze the thawed spinach to drain. While spinach
drains, melt the butter in a skillet over medium heat. Add
onion; sauté in butter until soft. Stir in the tomato pulp and
spinach. Cook, stirring constantly while spinach wilts
(approximately 3-4 minutes). Sprinkle in cheese, bread crumbs
and nutmeg; blend well.

Fill the tomato shells with the spinach mixture. Place in an
ungreased baking dish; sprinkle remaining Parmesan over tops
of tomatoes. At this point tomatoes may be refrigerated for
several hours. Allow the tomatoes to come to room
temperature before baking.

Preheat oven to broil.

Tomatoes should be at least 4 inches from broiler unit. Broil
until cheese is slightly browned (approximately 4-5 minutes).
Remove from oven.

Serve broiled stuffed tomatoes immediately. Garnish each
with fresh dill sprigs.

8 servings

Jane O'Kelley finds that
these stuffed tomatoes are
a simple, yet elegant
accompaniment to any
luncheon or dinner. They can
be stuffed, refrigerated and
brought to room temperature
before broiling and serving.
Lay individual servings on a
lettuce leaf and garnish the top
of each with a fresh dill sprig.

*To skin a tomato, spear the
stem end with a fork and dip it into
a saucepan of boiling water for
several seconds. Lift it out of the
water, slit the skin with a small
knife and peel it off.*

Sliced Tomatoes with Pesto Vinaigrette

3 ripe tomatoes, sliced to
  1/4 inch thickness
1/4 cup red wine vinegar
1/2 cup olive oil

4 tablespoons PESTO
1 clove garlic, minced
parsley for garnish

Arrange sliced tomatoes on serving plate. Combine vinegar, oil, pesto and garlic. Mix well. Drizzle dressing sparingly over the sliced tomatoes.

Chill for at least 15 minutes before serving. Garnish with parsley. Our recipe for PESTO is given along with our Fettucine recipe on page 99.

8 servings

Nothing surpasses vine ripened tomatoes fresh from the garden. Try serving them at the height of the season, sliced and drizzled with this pesto vinaigrette.

It is said that it was the magic of pesto that brought home the great seafarers of the ancient Mediterranean.

Marinated Green Beans and Mushrooms

1 pound mushrooms
1 pound green beans
1 cup olive oil
4 tablespoons tarragon
  vinegar

1/4 teaspoon salt
black pepper to taste
2 1/2 teaspoons minced
  parsley
3/4 teaspoon tarragon

Rinse, pat dry, and halve fresh mushrooms. Cut green beans into 1-inch pieces; set aside.

Bring a large pot of water to boiling. Add green beans; return to boiling point. Reduce heat; cover and simmer for 5 to 8 minutes or until tender. Add mushrooms and simmer for 2 minutes longer. Remove from heat, drain and cool.

In a large bowl combine olive oil, vinegar, salt, pepper, parsley and tarragon. Mix vegetables into olive oil mixture and let stand for 5 hours before serving.

6 servings

A great little side dish to serve at room temperature.

Cauliflower Sauté

2 tablespoons butter

4 cups sliced cauliflower

1 cup thinly sliced celery

1 tablespoon dried minced onion

1 tablespoon seasoned chicken stock base

1/2 cup dry white wine

1 teaspoon Mei Yen seasoning

salt and pepper to taste

Melt the butter in a large skillet. Add cauliflower, celery and onion.

In a small bowl combine chicken stock base with wine. Add Mei Yen, salt and pepper. Pour over vegetables in skillet.

Cook vegetables over medium high heat. Turn constantly with a wide spatula until vegetables are barely tender yet crisp. This will take approximately 7 minutes.

Serve at once.

4 servings

Mei Yen is found in the spice section of supermarkets.

The seasonings in this vegetable dish create an assertive flavor which heightens the taste of the cauliflower and celery.

Cauliflower is a type of cabbage that is encouraged to flower rather than produce leaves. Actually, the head is a mass of unopened flowers that is sometimes called the curd.

To prevent the vegetable from darkening during cooking add 1/2 cup milk to the water in which it is cooking.

Asparagus with Raspberry Mousseline

1 1/4 cups fresh raspberries or
   1 (10 ounce) package
   frozen raspberries, thawed
2 tablespoons raspberry
   vinegar
2 tablespoons lemon juice

1/2 cup olive oil
1/4 teaspoon nutmeg
1/4 teaspoon salt
1/2 cup heavy cream,
   whipped
2 pounds fresh asparagus

Purée and strain raspberries. Add raspberry vinegar and lemon juice to purée. Blend in olive oil, nutmeg and salt. Fold in whipped cream. Refrigerate until serving.

Steam asparagus until tender and bright green (approximately 7 minutes). Remove to a warm platter.

Spoon mousseline over steamed asparagus just before serving.

8 servings

This unusual dish is not only striking in appearance but easy to use for entertaining. Make the mousseline early in the day and take it out of the refrigerator just before serving.

Springtime Asparagus

1 teaspoon arrowroot
2 tablespoons butter
1 teaspoon chicken stock base
*1 teaspoon Mei Yen seasoning
1/4 teaspoon lemon peel

1/4 teaspoon basil
2 tomatoes, coarsely
   chopped
1 pound fresh asparagus

In a small dish blend arrowroot with 1/2 cup water; set aside.

Melt butter in a small pan. Add chicken stock base, Mei Yen, lemon peel, basil and arrowroot mixture. Cook over medium heat, stirring constantly until mixture boils and thickens. Add tomatoes to the sauce and cook the sauce for 2 to 3 minutes longer. Remove from heat and keep warm.

Trim off asparagus bottoms with a diagonal cut. Steam asparagus 7 minutes or until just tender and bright green. Turn asparagus onto a heated serving dish; cover with springtime sauce.

6 servings

*Although Mei Yen Seasoning is still manufactured by Spice Island Co., it has become increasingly difficult to find. We have found that you may substitute 1/4 teaspoon salt and 1/2 teaspoon sugar for the Mei Yen.

Asparagus is one of those crisp flavors we like to savor each spring. Freida Weaver uses this zesty blend of seasonings to enhance the fresh taste of the asparagus.

Thomas Jefferson grew asparagus in the greenhouses of Monticello.

Artichokes with Dips

4 artichokes
1 or more dipping sauces

Wash and trim artichokes. Line a vegetable steamer basket
with lemon slices and place basket in a 6-quart pot with
1 quart of water. Steam until tender (about 45 minutes).
Don't allow the pot to boil dry. Drain and chill.

Wreath a plate with several layers of cooked artichoke leaves.
Place a bowl of your choice of dip in the center of the wreath.

Our families look forward to
the arrival of fresh artichokes.
Serve hot or cold artichokes
with one or both of these zesty
sauces.

Curry Dip

1 cup mayonnaise
1 tablespoon fresh lemon juice
1 teaspoon curry powder
1/4 teaspoon minced garlic

Combine all ingredients and stir until well blended.

Olive and Cream Cheese Sauce

6 ounces cream cheese, softened
1/4 cup sour cream
2 teaspoons white wine vinegar
1/4 cup black olives, minced
1 clove garlic
salt to taste

*Artichokes cause an unusual
chemical reaction in the mouth
when eaten. Their nutty taste can
cause any subsequent food to taste
sweet. This reaction may alter the
taste of the chosen wine.*

Combine all ingredients in a blender or food processor to mix.
Chill before serving.

Hint: 1/2 teaspoon milk may be stirred into dip just before
serving to attain proper dipping consistency.

4 servings

Rockwell Baked Beans

2 cups beans
1/2 yellow onion, chopped
1/2 pound bacon, cut in pieces
1/4 cup sugar
1/2 teaspoon salt
1 tablespoon molasses
1-2 tablespoons ketchup

If the beans are fresh from a garden, they will not need to soak in water overnight. However, if you are using store bought beans, they need to be covered with water and left overnight.

On the following day, place the beans in a large kettle. Cover the beans with plenty of water; simmer them until desired firmness. (If salt is added to the beans, they will not soften further.)

In a frying pan, brown the onion and bacon. Drain and add to the beans. Add the sugar, salt, molasses and ketchup to the beans. Simmer for 1 or 2 more hours.

8 servings

Elizabeth Hancock shares her own recipe for baked beans using the "Rockwell" bean which is grown in Coupeville. She describes the Rockwell as a small white bean with brown spots. Elizabeth suggests using pinto beans as a replacement to the Coupeville Rockwell.

"Here's a little history on Rockwell beans. Mr. Rockwell brought the beans from Kansas to Coupeville by horse and wagon. Only the local Coupeville farmers grow them now. Unfortunately, it's rather common for a crop to fail. Seeds must be grown from the previous year's crop; fresh seed is often generously passed around the local farmers. This has kept the Rockwells from oblivion. It's often heard, 'There's nothing like a Rockwell.'"

Broccoli Casserole

2 (10 ounce) packages frozen, chopped broccoli
1 tablespoon butter
1 cup milk
1 tablespoon flour
salt and pepper to taste
3 whole eggs
2/3 cup mayonnaise
1 tablespoon minced onion flakes
1 cup grated cheddar cheese

Preheat oven to 350°.

Thaw, cook and drain broccoli. Set aside.

To prepare basic white sauce melt butter in a small pan. Add milk and whisk in flour. Cook over medium heat, stirring constantly until thick. Remove from heat. Add salt and pepper to taste.

Beat eggs in a large bowl. Add mayonnaise and onion. Blend in white sauce. Combine broccoli with egg mixture and mix together.

Pour mixture into a 9 x 13-inch buttered casserole. Cover with grated cheese and bake at 350° for 30 minutes. Center of casserole should be firm before removing from oven.

Hint: This can be prepared 12 hours in advance and refrigerated. Bring to room temperature before baking.

8-10 servings

Sharon Solin's savory vegetable dish is a delightful discovery for the busy cook. It is easy to assemble and transport to any year-round buffet.

The origin of broccoli has been traced to Asia Minor, and was called Italian Asparagus when it first reached England in the 17th century. Broccoli was first brought to America by Italian immigrants.

Broccoli with Lemon Herb Sauce

1 egg
2 teaspoons Dijon mustard
1 1/2 tablespoons fresh lemon juice
3/4 cup vegetable oil
1 teaspoon grated lemon peel
2 tablespoons finely chopped fresh chives
1 tablespoon chopped fresh parsley
salt and pepper to taste
2 pounds broccoli

Whirl egg with mustard and lemon juice in an electric blender or food processor. With motor running, pour oil through feed tube in a slow, steady stream until all oil is incorporated. Add lemon peel, chives and parsley. Season to taste with salt and pepper. Refrigerate until serving.

Steam broccoli until tender, about 7 minutes. Drain.

Bring Lemon Herb Sauce to room temperature before spooning over individual servings of warm broccoli.

6 servings

Tangy Lemon Herb Sauce is delicious over fresh, steamed broccoli. We have also used the sauce drizzled over tiny new potatoes, or as a dip for artichokes and Turkish Fried Mussels.

Chives, the smallest member of the onion family, are one of the classic "fine herbes" and are essential to many herb sauces.

Stir Fry Snap Peas

2 cups sugar snap peas
1 tablespoon soy sauce
1 teaspoon cornstarch
1 tablespoon sherry wine

1 teaspoon sugar
1 tablespoon vegetable oil
1/2 cup sliced water
    chestnuts, drained

Remove strings from snap peas.

In a small bowl whisk soy sauce with cornstarch. Stir in 3 tablespoons water, sherry, and sugar and set aside.

Heat a wok or large skillet. Add oil. Stir fry peas lifting with a spatula in an "up and over" motion for approximately 3 minutes or until tender.

Stir soy mixture and add to wok. Cook and stir until thickened. Add water chestnuts, cover, and cook 1 minute more. Serve immediately.

4 servings

Garden fresh peas taste much different than the canned or frozen peas you may have grown up with. Sugar Snap Peas have a plump, vivid green pod that contains fully developed peas. They actually require very little cooking time, so stir frying suits them best. They are also delicious when nibbled right off the vine. To retain their fullest flavor, Sugar Snaps should be used within a day or two of harvesting.

Purée of Peas

2 cups shelled large peas
butter

salt and pepper to taste
freshly grated nutmeg for garnish

Boil peas until tender. Drain peas in a colander, reserving liquid. Force peas through food mill, strainer, or purée in a food processor. Moisten peas with reserved liquid. The purée should be thicker than soup, but thinner than mashed potatoes.

Return purée to saucepan, season with butter, salt and pepper; stir to blend. Warm gently over low heat.

Grate fresh nutmeg over individual servings.

4 servings

Here is a new twist to utilizing those large forgotten peas on summer vines. Ruby Thomas shared this recipe with us.

Coconut Baked Sweet Potatoes

10 medium size sweet potatoes
1/3 cup butter
3/4 cup brown sugar
1/2 cup flaked coconut

Glaze: 1/4 cup butter
   1/2 cup brown sugar
   1/4 cup heavy cream
   3/4 cup coconut

Joyce DeJong prepares this tasty alternative to the traditional sweet potato.

One day before serving, cook the sweet potatoes in boiling water until almost tender (approximately 20 minutes). Drain, cool, peel and cut them in half lengthwise. Arrange the potatoes in a greased 9 x 13-inch baking dish.

In a small saucepan over medium heat melt the butter, brown sugar and 1/4 cup water. Pour this over the cooked potatoes. Cover the potatoes and allow them to stand overnight.

On the day of serving, sprinkle the coconut over the potatoes.

Preheat oven to 350°.

To prepare the glaze, combine the butter, brown sugar and cream in a small saucepan. Melt over medium heat until the glaze is smooth. Pour the glaze over the potatoes.

Bake in a 350° oven to heat thoroughly. Sprinkle remaining coconut over the potatoes just before serving.

12 servings

Potatoes with Rosemary and Garlic

10-12 large potatoes, peeled
3 tablespoons olive oil
3 tablespoons butter
3 teaspoons rosemary
3 cloves garlic, minced
1/2 teaspoon salt
ground pepper to taste

Using a melon baller, scoop potatoes into balls. Fill a large saucepan half full with salted water. Bring to a boil and add potatoes. Allow water to return to a boil for 5 minutes before draining potatoes in a colander. When drained, place them on paper towels to dry.

Melt oil and butter together in a large skillet. Add drained potatoes along with rosemary, garlic, salt and pepper. Cook over medium heat turning to brown on all sides.

8 servings

Turn an ordinary vegetable into something unique. Try the innovative preparation of this potato dish, and savor the distinctive flavor of garlic.

Rosemary is a great herb to grow because it is an evergreen; therefore the herb is always available fresh. It will thrive in any dry, warm place and blossom with pretty pale, blue flowers providing a sweet aroma.

Orange Rice

3 tablespoons butter
2/3 cup diced celery, with leaves
2 tablespoons chopped onion
1 cup fresh orange juice
grated rind from 1 orange
1 1/4 teaspoons salt
1/4 teaspoon thyme
1 cup uncooked white rice

Melt the butter in a medium size saucepan. Add celery and onion; cook until onion is soft and golden. Add 1 1/2 cups water, orange juice, rind, salt and thyme. Bring to a boil. Add rice slowly, stirring constantly. Cover; reduce heat and simmer for 25 minutes or until rice is tender.

Remove from heat and keep the rice covered until time to serve.

6 servings

The subtle citrus flavor and color of orange in the rice make it a refreshing accompaniment to a fish or poultry entrée.

Deception Pass Bridge is one of the most photographed attractions in Washington. This spectacular site attracts millions of visitors each year. The Bridge was built in 1935 for about $315,000 and it stretches 1,487 feet in length. The structure straddles Deception Pass, a treacherous, narrow passage of water that has fascinated people since its discovery by Joseph Whidbey in 1792.

Six Persimmons Fried Rice

5 tablespoons vegetable oil

3 eggs, slightly beaten

1/2 cup diced barbequed pork, ham, or small shrimp

6 or more large mushrooms, sliced

4 green onions, chopped

1 stalk celery with leaves, chopped

4 cups cooked rice

1 teaspoon salt

1/2 teaspoon pepper

1/2 teaspoon Accent

2 tablespoons soy sauce

Heat 1 tablespoon oil in skillet. Scramble the eggs until done. Use a spatula to cut eggs into small pieces. Set aside.

Heat remaining 4 tablespoons oil. Stir fry the meat, mushrooms, onions and celery for 1 minute. Add rice, eggs, seasonings, and soy sauce to meat and vegetables. Stir fry until the rice is hot (about 5 minutes).

Serve fried rice immediately.

8 servings

This fried rice dish is one of many recipes that students learn to prepare in cooking classes offered at the *Six Persimmons*, located in Coupeville. Rose Brosseau instructs students about the Chinese method of food preparation which combines diverse flavors, textures and spices.

Tsao-Chun is the kitchen god of ancient China. It is during the Chinese New Year that Tsao-Chun looks in on the household. Children are told that Tsao-Chun goes to heaven to report his findings, so the children leave big pieces of molasses candy for him to find. Thus, when Tsao-Chun makes his report, he will only speak sweet words.

Admiralty Head Lighthouse

Lazy Day Picnic at Concerts on the Cove, Coupeville

The waters of Penn Cove are the backdrop to the stage in Coupeville's Town Park where "Concerts on the Cove" draws young and old alike to enjoy a variety of concerts throughout the summer months. The audience comes prepared with their own lawn chairs or blankets and often a delicious picnic to nibble on while the strains of delightful music fill the air.

Victorian Cheese Dip with Fruit

Pacific Flank Steak

Marinated Carrots

Smoked Salmon Rice Salad

Chocolate Raspberry Meringue Bars

Dixieland Jazz Festival

Experience Dixieland magic when you participate in the special events the Whidbey Island Dixieland Jazz Festival provides. Oak Harbor hosts several Dixieland bands and presents three days of rip roaring fun. Take advantage of the waterfront beer garden, the Sunday breakfast and gospel service. Strut your stuff on the large wooden dance floor overlooking the picturesque Oak Harbor bay and the marina.

The Dixieland Festival is the primary fundraiser for the Oak Harbor Kiwanis Club giving the club an opportunity to donate money to community programs.

Warm Crab Dip

Red Beans and Rice

Green Salad with Purple Chive Flowers

Marinated Green Beans and Mushrooms

White Cloud Pie

Rabbit Hunter's Style

1 (3 pound) rabbit
salt and pepper to taste
5 bacon slices
5 shallots, chopped
4 garlic cloves, minced
2 tablespoons flour
1 teaspoon thyme
1 teaspoon basil

1 1/2 cups dry white wine
1 (8 ounce) can tomato sauce
1 cup sliced mushrooms
snipped parsley for garnish

The *Kasteel Franssen* is a lovely restaurant in Oak Harbor that has been built in the old European style. It is easily recognized by the large, slow moving water wheel in front and the glittering white lights that outline the building. The atmosphere is warm and romantic as you dine by the fireplace and enjoy the subtle piano music.

Mike Franssen finds that this rabbit dish, "Lapin Sauté Chasseur," is a popular item on his menu.

Cut the rabbit into the following 12 pieces: 2 front legs; the saddle or back into 4 pieces; 2 back legs (each cut into 2 pieces); and the 2 rib pieces. Sprinkle the pieces of rabbit with salt and pepper.

In a large and heavy skillet, brown the bacon until crisp. Remove the bacon from the pan, reserving the bacon fat. Dry and crumble the bacon. Set aside.

Sauté the rabbit pieces in the skillet with the bacon fat. Brown all pieces evenly. Remove the rabbit to an ovenproof dish and keep warm in a 200° oven.

Add the shallots and garlic to the skillet in which the rabbit was browned. Sauté for 1 minute. Sprinkle in the flour, thyme and basil and stir well. Deglaze with the wine for 1 minute. Add 1 1/2 cups water and the tomato sauce.

Place the rabbit pieces back in the skillet. Cover and cook over low heat for 40 minutes.

Add the sliced mushrooms to the rabbit, cover again and cook for 15 more minutes or until the rabbit is tender.

Serve the Rabbit Hunter's Style garnished with freshly snipped parsley. Rice or new potatoes work well as accompaniments.

6 servings

Glazed Cornish Game Hens

4 Cornish game hens
3 cups bread crumbs
1 tablespoon lemon juice
1/4 cup dried currants
2 tablespoons freshly minced parsley
1/2 teaspoon salt
1/4 cup butter, melted

Glaze: 1/4 cup red currant jelly
        1/4 cup orange juice
        1/4 cup butter, melted

Preheat oven to 350°.

Rinse and dry hens.

In a large bowl, combine the bread crumbs, lemon juice, currants, parsley, salt and butter for stuffing. Stuff the birds and close them with pins or sew them shut.

Mix the glaze ingredients in a small saucepan and simmer for 5 minutes. Lightly brush each hen with the glaze.

Place the hens in a large oven roasting pan and bake at 350° for 1 hour. Brush the hens with the glaze at 15-minute intervals. The hens may also be cooked by roasting them on a spit for 1 hour. When the meat is done it will easily pull away from the bone. Remove the game hens to a serving platter and serve 1 hen per person.

4 servings

Chris Skinner, our number one taster, editor and legal counsel, provides one of his favorite recipes.

Discover one of Whidbey Island's best kept secrets: Whidbey Island Vineyard. Greg and Elizabeth Osenbach have spent 6 years developing a vineyard full of "vinefera" grapes. The grapes are plump, yet firm and they thrive beautifully in Whidbey Island's marine climate. We had an opportunity to taste their dry white wine, "Madeline Angevine." This is a first class wine and a perfect compliment to any meal. Whidbey Island Vineyard should definitely be one of your stops between north and south Whidbey. Their tasting room will be open to visitors in early 1992.

Chicken Loganberry

4 boneless chicken breasts, without skin
2 tablespoons olive oil
2 cups Whidbeys Loganberry wine
1 cup heavy cream
flour for dredging chicken

Preheat oven to 325°.

Pound each chicken breast flat between 2 pieces of plastic wrap. Lightly dredge the breasts in flour. In a skillet over medium high heat, warm olive oil. Sauté chicken breasts on each side until lightly browned. Remove chicken from the skillet and place in a baking dish to keep warm in a preheated oven at 325°.

Before cleaning the skillet, add the wine to the skillet and heat on high. Boil the wine until the amount is reduced by two-thirds. Add the cream and bring to a boil. Reduce sauce by half. The sauce should be thick and smooth.

To serve, pour the loganberry sauce over the breasts.

4 servings

Christopher Panek takes great pride in the food he presents to those who dine in his quaint restaurant, *Christopher's*, in Coupeville. Serve Chicken Loganberry to utilize and enjoy the deep, rich flavor of Whidbey Island's loganberry.

The world's largest loganberry farm is located at the narrowest spot on Whidbey Island, from where you can see both the east and west shores.

The Loganberry Farm, Whidbey's, is operated by Ste. Michelle Vintners, Inc. The farm is producing Whidbeys Liqueur and Loganberry wine. It also offers self-guided tours and a complimentary tasting bar.

Norman's Watermark Sandwiches

Chicken Marinade

1 cup olive oil
juice from 1 large lemon
2 tablespoons freshly snipped parsley
4-5 minced garlic cloves
1/2 teaspoon coarse ground black pepper
salt to taste
6 chicken breasts, skinned and boned

Mix all the ingredients in a shallow baking dish. Add the chicken breasts. Cover and store in a refrigerator overnight.

Sandwich ingredients and instructions

6 sourdough French rolls or hoagie rolls
butter or olive oil for spreading
fresh cilantro
1 (7 ounce) can whole green chiles
8 ounces Monterey Jack cheese
mayonnaise for spreading

Grill the breasts, brushing with the marinade, until they are nearly done (about 7 minutes per side). Slice the rolls in half and brush the insides of the rolls with the butter or olive oil. Place the rolls near the coals to warm them. Wash and dry the cilantro, open and drain the chiles, and slice the cheese to fit the breasts.

When the breasts are nearly done and nicely browned, top each one with a cheese slice. While the cheese melts, spread the mayonnaise on the rolls. Place a chicken breast on each roll and add a whole chile to each breast. Top with fresh cilantro leaves. Cover with the top half of the roll. Slice the roll in half and serve.

6 servings

Norman Sturdevant prepares his outstanding main course sandwiches on an outdoor grill. To accompany the marinated chicken sandwiches, he heats individually wrapped ears of corn on the same grill. Add a pat of butter to each cob and turn them frequently as you baste the chicken with the marinade.

Hot foods will retain heat for several hours if wrapped in several layers of aluminum foil and then in newspapers as soon as they are removed from the oven.

Coq au Vin

3 fryer chickens, cut up
1/2 cup margarine
3 1/2 cups dry red wine
1/4 teaspoon thyme
2 teaspoons salt
1/2 teaspoon rosemary
1 bay leaf
1 tablespoon chicken stock base
3 cloves garlic, minced

1 1/2 pounds fresh
   mushrooms, sliced
1 1/2 tablespoons lemon
   juice
8 slices bacon
2 (15 ounce) cans small
   whole, white
   onions, drained
2 (15 ounce) cans new
   potatoes, drained

When entertaining a large group of people in your home, prepare this hearty "French country" entrée.

In a large frying pan, brown the chicken in 1/4 cup butter. Pour in the wine to loosen the browned drippings. Transfer chicken and liquid to a large "Dutch oven" type pan with a cover. Add the thyme, salt, rosemary, bay leaf, chicken stock base and garlic to the chicken. Stir in the seasonings until well blended. Cover chicken and simmer for 1 hour, until chicken is barely tender.

While the chicken cooks, sauté the mushroom caps and stems in a pan with the remaining 1/4 cup butter and lemon juice. After a few minutes transfer all of this to the pan with the chicken.

In the same pan in which you sautéed the mushrooms, cook the bacon until browned. Remove the bacon from the pan and drain on paper towels. Reserve 2 tablespoons of the bacon grease in the pan.

Place the onions in the pan with the 2 tablespoons bacon grease. Sprinkle the onions with sugar; heat and lightly brown. Add the onions to the chicken.

Place the potatoes and crumbled bacon in the pan with the chicken.

Cover the pan of chicken. At this point the chicken may be refrigerated for several hours before serving. Before serving, warm the chicken in a 350° oven until all is heated through.

12 servings

In order to retain fresh mushrooms, refrigerate them and keep them covered with a damp paper towel. Do not keep them in plastic bags as they require air circulation and humidity.

Stuffed Chicken Breast with Red Wine Sauce

4 whole chicken breasts, skinned, boned and halved
salt and pepper to taste
1 teaspoon tarragon
8 thin slices prosciutto ham
8 tablespoons CREAMY GARLIC CHEESE, (or
    prepared cheese such as Alouette or Boursin)
4 tablespoons white wine

Red Wine Sauce

Preheat oven to 450°.

Sprinkle each chicken breast half with salt, pepper and
tarragon. Place a slice of prosciutto and 1 tablespoon creamy
cheese in the center of each breast. Wrap the chicken around
the ham and cheese; secure with a toothpick and place seam-
side-down in a buttered casserole dish.

Pour white wine over breasts and cook at 450° for 20 minutes
or until golden brown. Pass Red Wine Sauce to be spooned
over each serving.

Red Wine Sauce

2 tablespoons butter	1/2 cup red wine
1 cup chopped green onion	2 cups BEEF STOCK
1 teaspoon garlic	1 teaspoon worcestershire
1 cup sliced mushrooms	sauce
3 tablespoons flour	pinch of cayenne pepper

Sauté onion, garlic and mushrooms in butter. Add flour and
cook 3 minutes. Add red wine, beef stock, worcestershire and
cayenne; cook until thickened.

8 servings

Celebrate a special occasion
by serving this elegant entrée.

*Tarragon originated in the
Middle East. It is an herb with
many uses such as providing an
appetizing aroma when added to
a barbeque fire. It can also be
frozen in ice cubes to use in
flavoring cold drinks.*

Chicken Parmesan on Pasta

4 whole chicken breasts, skinned, boned and halved
2 (14 1/2 ounce) cans Italian style stewed tomatoes
2 tablespoons cornstarch
3/4 teaspoon oregano
1/3 cup freshly grated Parmesan cheese
Fettucine or Angel Hair pasta
fresh parsley or cilantro for garnish

Preheat oven to 425°.

Arrange chicken breasts in a baking dish. Cover and bake for 15 minutes at 425°. Remove the chicken from the oven and drain. In a saucepan combine tomatoes, cornstarch and oregano. Stir constantly until mixture has thickened. Pour heated sauce over chicken. Top with Parmesan. Bake 5 minutes, uncovered.

Prepare Fettucine or Angel Hair pasta according to package instructions.

On each individual plate, arrange a chicken breast with sauce on top of pasta. Garnish with parsley or cilantro and more Parmesan, if desired.

6-8 servings

Kim Skinner's Chicken Parmesan on Pasta was an instant success in our households. The cook will appreciate the ease with which it is prepared and your families will enjoy its attractive presentation and full flavor.

Pasta, rice and some vegetables should be cooked "al dente." This Italian term, meaning "to the tooth," describes foods that are not overcooked, but are firm to the bite.

Artichoke Chicken Manicotti

2 cups cooked chicken

2 cups grated mozzarella cheese

1 (6 ounce) jar marinated artichoke hearts
(reserve liquid)

1 (4 ounce) can mushroom pieces, drained

1/2 cup undiluted cream of mushroom soup

1/4 cup grated Romano cheese

1 garlic clove, minced

4 cups TOMATO SAUCE

1/2 cup white wine

10-12 manicotti shells

Combine chicken, mozzarella, artichoke hearts and mushrooms in a large bowl. Mix together the reserved liquid from the artichokes, soup, Romano cheese and garlic. Pour over chicken mixture and blend well.

Cook manicotti according to package directions until it is barely tender. Flush with cold water.

Preheat oven to 375°.

Pour 2 cups of the tomato sauce in the bottom of a 2-quart baking dish, or a 9 x 13-inch pan. Fill manicotti shells with chicken mixture and place over tomato sauce in baking dish. Add white wine and any leftover chicken and artichoke mixture to the remaining tomato sauce; mix well. Pour over the manicotti.

Bake at 375° for 1 hour.

Serve manicotti on warmed plates.

8 servings

Our fresh tomato sauce highlights this Artichoke Chicken Manicotti from the kitchen of Melissa Zylstra.

Artichokes are cultivated where the climate is cool, foggy and free of frost.

Fettucine al Pesto

1 cup heavy cream
1/2 cup half and half
1 1/2 cups grated Parmesan
cheese
1/2 cup butter

2 egg yolks, beaten
salt and white pepper to taste
1 teaspoon olive oil
1 pound fettucine

1/2 cup Pesto Sauce

Heat the cream and half and half over medium heat. When it begins to simmer, sprinkle the cheese in a little at a time, stirring after each addition. Lower heat and continue to stir mixture for 10 minutes. Add butter, one tablespoon at a time.

Stir until butter is well incorporated. Remove sauce from heat and pour 1/4 cup sauce into small bowl with beaten eggs. Beat with a whisk and then return egg mixture to the remaining sauce in pan. Season to taste with salt and white pepper.

To 4 cups boiling salted water, add 1 teaspoon olive oil and fettucine noodles. Boil noodles until they are barely tender. Drain and rinse quickly with cold water. Allow pasta to drain again. Immediately add fettucine noodles to sauce and stir until just mixed. Spoon fettucine on to individual warmed plates and top each serving with a heaping tablespoon of pesto sauce.

Pesto Sauce

2 cups firmly packed fresh
basil leaves
1/4 cup pine nuts
3 cloves garlic, peeled

3/4 cup freshly grated
Parmesan cheese
1/2 cup olive oil

Wash basil leaves and dry completely between paper towels. In an electric blender, whirl basil leaves, pine nuts and garlic until puréed. Blend in cheese. With machine on low speed, pour oil in slowly to blend.

If not serving immediately, cover pesto with a thin layer of olive oil to prevent darkening. Refrigerate.

4 servings

For a delicious dinner with an Italian theme, serve this fettucine after treating your guests to "Seabolt's Smoked Salmon Antipasto." A fresh Italian bread would complete the meal nicely.

Pesto will keep about one week in the refrigerator. The surface will darken when exposed to air, but just give it a stir before using. A clean dry ice cube tray makes a handy container for freezing pesto. Store frozen pesto cubes in a plastic bag or airtight container.

Pesto is usually served on pasta but is equally palatable when dolloped in vegetable soups, added to vinaigrette dressing, or spooned over broiled fish.

Spaghetti Alla Amalfitana

6-8 slices cooked American ham, cut in strips
2 cloves garlic, minced
1 1/2 tablespoons olive oil
1/4 cup white wine
2 cups chopped tomatoes or TOMATO SAUCE
salt to taste
3 tablespoons grated Parmesan cheese
1/2 cup sour cream (*panna per cucinare*)
1/4 cup cubed mozzarella cheese (*fior di latte*)
1 pound spaghetti

Brown the ham and garlic in olive oil in a saucepan over medium heat (about 3 minutes). Add wine; reduce heat to low. Stir in the tomatoes, salt and Parmesan; heat through.

Cook spaghetti noodles according to package directions.

Just before serving, add the sour cream and mozzarella. Heat through. Mix half of the sauce with the spaghetti and serve the remaining sauce at the table.

Offer freshly grated Parmesan cheese at the table for topping Spaghetti Alla Amalfitana.

6 servings

Some of the finest food in the world originates from northern Italy. While living there, Carol Dearth gathered an abundance of knowledge about the local population and their favorite pastime ... cooking. In Carol's house this recipe is called "Spaghetti with Pink Sauce."

The sauce is lightly colored, streaked with cheese and brimming with the essential flavor of fresh garlic. Carol often makes the sauce in advance so it can be frozen in ice cube trays.

When buying garlic make sure you purchase cloves that are free of spots and firm. Do not chill garlic as the moisture encourages sprouting. Raw garlic has a strong taste, but it is much more mild when cooked. Occasionally garlic may leave an unpleasant aftertaste. Chlorophyll is the antidote for this, so munch on a bite of parsley!

Red Beans and Rice

1 pound red beans

2 tablespoons margarine

1 cup diced white onion

1/4 cup chopped green onion

4 large cloves garlic, minced

1/2 pound Kielbasa sausage

1 pound cooked ham

1 teaspoon Creole seasoning

1 teaspoon pepper

1/8 teaspoon crushed red pepper flakes

1 tablespoon minced parsley

2 cups long grain rice, uncooked

Soak beans in 6 cups water overnight.

Melt margarine in a skillet over medium heat. Cook onion, green onion and garlic in margarine until soft. Chop sausage and ham into bite size pieces. Add to onions in skillet and brown lightly. Strain red beans.

Place beans, onions, ham and sausage in a large pot. Add 4 cups fresh water. Bring to a boil and add Creole seasoning, pepper, red pepper flakes and parsley. Reduce to simmer and cook for 3 hours. Stir beans occasionally and add more water if mixture appears to be too dry. Consistency should resemble a thick gravy.

Prepare rice according to package directions. Serve the red beans spooned over individual mounds of rice.

8 servings

Whidbey Island attracts inhabitants from all over the country and the world. This diverse population provides the source of a wide variety of "regional recipes" to add to the flavor of Whidbey.

Greer Moore brought this favorite with him when he moved to the Northwest many years ago from New Orleans.

In this recipe we have substituted Kielbasa sausage for the Andouille sausage which is traditionally used in New Orleans. Andouille sausage is not usually available in local markets. Creole seasoning is available in the seasoning section at most supermarkets. No salt was added to this recipe because the seasonings and meat provide enough salty flavor for our tastes.

Pizza Pattee with alternate toppings

2 envelopes (1/4 ounce) dry yeast	1 teaspoon salt
7 cups bread flour	1/4 cup olive oil

Stir yeast into 1/2 cup warm water and let sit for 10 minutes. Add 1 cup flour to form a soft starter dough. Cover with a cloth and let rest in a warm place for about an hour. Add 1 1/2 cups water, salt and olive oil, mixing well. Start adding the flour, 1 cup at a time until the dough becomes too stiff to stir. Turn it out on a floured board and continue kneading in the rest of the flour. Knead for about 10 minutes. As you knead, the dough should become smoother and more elastic.

Divide the dough into six portions. Place dough balls on a floured surface and cover with a cloth. This rising will take from 1 to 2 hours, and the dough should double in size. At this time punch them down and knead each into a circle.

Stretch the dough on a floured surface making 6 round pizza shells.

Preheat oven to 400°.

After topping, each pizza should be baked for 16-20 minutes or until bubbly. Watch closely.

Now the creativity begins. Your friends can design their own pizzas or you can serve several different pizza entrées. Here are some of Patti's favorite toppings.

Pizza with Oil and Garlic

Brush dough with olive oil. Sprinkle on 6 to 12 sliced garlic cloves. Add salt and pepper. A variation is to add basil or fresh herbs to the above.

Pizza with Tomato and Basil

Peel and seed about 4 medium tomatoes. Cover dough with tomatoes and a handful of chopped basil. Moisten with a tiny bit of olive oil sprinkled over all toppings. Add salt and pepper to taste.

Patti Pattee enjoys creating pizza from scratch. The toppings Patti uses are unusual, nutritious and full flavored. The baking pizza will fill your kitchen with aromas that are hard to resist.

continued on next page

Pizza with Onions

Thinly slice one onion and spread slices over dough. Moisten with oil. Sprinkle on 1/4 cup Romano cheese. Top with freshly ground pepper.

Quattro Formaggio (Four Cheeses)

Choose any four cheeses, such as Mozzarella, Gruyère, Provolone, Pecorino or Gorgonzola. Grate cheeses. Spread over dough and sprinkle with pepper.

Quattro Stagione (Four Seasons)

Visually divide the dough into fourths and put a different ingredient on each section. Some suggestions include mushrooms, olives, peppers, cheese, sausage, capers, prosciutto and even seafood.

Paruskys

2 loaves frozen bread dough, thawed

2 medium onions, chopped

2 tablespoons butter

2 pounds extra lean hamburger

1 teaspoon salt

1/2 teaspoon garlic salt

2 tablespoons chopped parsley

2 tablespoons milk

This adaptation of a Polish classic, "Pierogi," is easy to make and is a great brown bag item for skiing or sailing trips. They are tasty when eaten hot or cold.

In a large skillet, sauté onions in butter until golden. Add hamburger, stirring to crumble. Add salt, garlic salt and parsley. Cook until meat is browned. Drain well.

Preheat oven to 400°.

Slice bread dough into 12 pieces. Roll each slice into a 6-inch round. Place 2 tablespoons of meat mixture on each round. Bring sides together and seal, making plump centers with tapered ends.

Place bundles seam-side-down on 2 well greased baking sheets. Brush tops with milk and bake at 400° for 20 minutes.

12 Paruskys

Lowell's Dogs

12 all beef wieners, not giant sized
12 Wonder Buns
1 1/2 pounds extra lean hamburger
1 (4 ounce) can tomato paste
1 (1.25 ounce) can chili powder
1 envelope coleslaw mix
1 (16 ounce) package prepared cabbage for coleslaw
1 large onion, chopped
mustard

In a medium pan bring 3 cups water to a boil. When water is boiling rapidly, add wieners, cover the pan and remove from heat. Let stand 5 minutes and drain.

Brown hamburger and drain fat. Add tomato paste, chili powder and a small amount of water to moisten hamburger; warm over low temperature.

To prepare coleslaw pour the contents of the coleslaw mix into a small bowl. Following the directions on the back of the envelope adding only half of the amount of sugar and vinegar called for. Pour this mixture over cut cabbage and add only enough mayonnaise to moisten cabbage.

To assemble Lowell's Dogs, spread warm buns with a small amount of mustard. Spread 1 tablespoon of chili mixture over each bun. Spread with the back of the spoons so that a thin layer of chili completely covers the bun. Sprinkle liberally with onion. Place cooked wieners over chili and fill with coleslaw.

Wrap each hotdog in waxed paper. Place all wrapped hotdogs on a baking sheet and place in the oven on low heat.

According to Dave, if the chili or coleslaw is too moist the hotdog becomes a soggy "clog." He advised us that "no garnish is needed. These babies stand on their own."

12 servings

Dave Harrington has carried on a family tradition of serving his father's famous "dogs" and all the trimmings. When we asked Dave to share his recipe he was adamant as to the ingredients used and the method of preparation.

We urge you to try these great hotdogs at your next gathering whether it be a backyard bash or a post-game huddle around the fireplace.

Stuffed Burgers

1 1/2 pounds lean ground beef

Filling:
1 green pepper, chopped
1 small bunch green onions, chopped (including tops)
1 cup grated cheddar cheese
1 (2 1/4 ounce) can chopped black olives
2 tablespoons mayonnaise

Hamburger buns and condiments

Divide the beef into 8 parts and shape into patties (do not squeeze all the juice from the beef).

In a bowl mix together all filling ingredients.

Place a generous portion of filling on top of 4 single patties. Cover each with the remaining 4 patties, pressing the edges of each to secure the filling.

Grill, barbeque or broil the burgers to desired doneness.

Serve each stuffed burger on large hamburger buns with assorted condiments.

4 servings

Bud Skinner grills these extra thick stuffed patties on the deck of *Fatal Attraction*, while cruising with his family.

Fort Ebey on North Whidbey Island was built in response to the Japanese air attacks on Pearl Harbor. The fort was designed to be invisible from enemy aircraft. In 1946 the fort was abandoned by the military and most of the fort's support buildings were dismantled. At that time the fort was donated to the Washington Park system. Today Fort Ebey is part of a growing 226-acre state park with more than three miles of hiking trails, 15 picnic sites and 53 campsites.

Spud Stew

1 pound beef, cut up in stew size bites
4 tablespoons olive oil
6-8 red potatoes
1 large yellow onion
5-6 large tomatoes, or 1 (14 ounce) can tomatoes
1 box Knorr's Oxtail Soup Mix
3-4 tablespoons freshly chopped parsley
2 teaspoons ground thyme, or 1 fresh thyme leaf
1 teaspoon coarsely ground pepper
3-4 cloves garlic, minced
1 (10 1/2 ounce) can beef consomme, or 1 1/2 cups
    BEEF STOCK

Preheat the oven to 250°.

Season the beef, according to taste, and lightly dredge in flour. In a large kettle, sauté the beef in the olive oil, and drain.

Cut the potatoes, onion and the tomatoes into large bite size pieces and add the vegetables to the beef.

In another bowl combine the soup mix with 4 cups cold water. Add the parsley, thyme, pepper, garlic and consomme, or beef stock. Blend thoroughly and add this to the beef in the kettle.

Bake the stew in a 250° oven for 4 hours.

Serve Spud Stew while it is hot, accompanied with bread for dipping into the broth.

8 servings

Warm up on Whidbey's blustery days with Jane Mays' recipe for a nourishing winter time stew. This stew is especially popular when Jane and Byron "Spud" Skubi host their annual apple squeeze party at their home on Penn Cove. Put out baskets of bread and blocks of cheese to accompany the stew.

The onion is actually a bulb in the lily family. There are many groups of onions – sweet, red, white, scallions, shallots, chives and leeks. The key to fresh onions is storage in a dark place with cool air circulation.

Mexican Curry

1 pound lean ground beef

1 onion, chopped

salt, pepper and garlic powder to taste

1 1/2 cups cooked white rice

1 (15 ounce) can tomato sauce

1 tablespoon chili powder

1 teaspoon oregano

1 teaspoon curry powder

1 teaspoon sugar

1 bag corn chips

1 head lettuce, shredded

2 cups grated cheddar cheese

2 large tomatoes, chopped

1-2 (2 1/4 ounce) cans black olives, sliced

In a large skillet, brown the beef and onion with seasonings. Drain. Prepare the rice while the beef is cooking.

Add the tomato sauce, 1 cup water and remaining seasonings to the beef and blend together well. Lower heat and simmer the mixture for 30 minutes.

Add the cooked rice to the beef mixture; heat through.

On each plate layer the lettuce over some corn chips. Place Mexican Curry on top. Continue layering with the cheese, tomatoes, olives and any other garnish you desire.

8 servings

When faced with a last minute decision about what you should fix for dinner, try Joan Norman's quick and easy recipe for Mexican Curry. Layer this spicy dish, tostada style, over corn chips and a bed of lettuce.

Useless Bay on South Whidbey is the perfect place for nature lovers to explore. Described as a wetland, Useless Bay is a refuge site for many types of plant and animal life. More than 100 species of birds inhabit this area which contains a bay and tidal marshlands, ponds and many small grassy "islands."

Tex Mex Enchiladas

3 tablespoons bacon drippings

1 to 3 cloves garlic, minced

3 tablespoons flour

1 tablespoon cumin

1 teaspoon oregano

5-6 tablespoons chili powder

4 cups BEEF STOCK

1 pound ground beef, browned (optional)

8 ounces shredded longhorn cheese

8 ounces shredded Monterey Jack cheese

1 cup chopped onion

10 corn tortillas

oil for frying

To make the enchilada sauce, heat the bacon drippings in a frying pan and slowly sauté the garlic, flour, cumin and oregano until golden brown. Add the chili powder, stir in 1 cup stock and simmer for 2 minutes. Add remaining stock and ground beef if desired. Season with salt and pepper and simmer for 30 minutes.

Preheat oven to 350°.

Combine shredded cheeses and chopped onion.

In a skillet pour oil to 1 inch deep and heat to 375°. Dip corn tortillas one at a time into the oil very briefly to soften the tortillas. Place tortillas on a warm plate. Spread each tortilla with 1 tablespoon enchilada sauce and sprinkle with 3 tablespoons of the cheese mixture. Roll up and place in an ovenproof pan into which a layer of enchilada sauce has been poured. Continue filling and rolling tortillas and placing them side by side in the dish. Pour remaining enchilada sauce over the rolled tortillas. Sprinkle with remaining cheese.

Bake at 350° for 25 minutes.

6 servings

Steve Hazelrigg recommended this recipe for an informal gathering of big eaters.

"Those who dwell among the beauties and mysteries of the earth are never alone or weary of life. Those who contemplate the beauty of the earth find reserves of strength that will endure as long as life lasts."

– Rachel Carson

Oyster Sauce Beef

1 pound flank steak

4 tablespoons oil

3 tablespoons Oyster Sauce

1 teaspoon sugar

1 teaspoon salt

1/4 teaspoon pepper

1 teaspoon sherry wine

1 tablespoon cornstarch

1 medium size yellow onion, sliced in thin rings

2 cups cooked rice

Slice the flank steak in 1 1/2-inch long strips.

In a wok or frying pan, heat the oil and add the beef. Stir fry quickly (about 2 minutes).

In a small bowl use a wire whisk to thoroughly mix the Oyster Sauce, sugar, salt, pepper, sherry, cornstarch and 6 tablespoons water. Add the sauce to the beef in the wok and continue to stir fry until the sauce is heated and has thickened.

Add the onion and stir fry for 1 more minute.

Serve Oyster Sauce Beef over rice.

4 servings

On a recent sailing trip, Chris Skinner impressed *The Ship of Fools* sailing crew with this stir fry dish from the *Six Persimmons* in Coupeville.

"I must go down to the sea again, to the lonely sea and the sky, And all I ask is a tall ship and a star to steer her by."

– J. Masefield

Beef Fondue with Assorted Sauces

Warm 1 cup vegetable oil with 1/2 cup butter in the fondue pot. Serve 1/2 pound beef (such as flank steak or top sirloin), per person. Cube the beef in bite size pieces and place on a platter.

Mustard Dill Sauce

1/4 cup prepared Dijon mustard
2 tablespoons prepared white horseradish
1 1/2 teaspoons dill weed
1/3 cup mayonnaise

Mix all ingredients together; chill until serving in a sauce dish.

Herbed Mayonnaise

1 cup mayonnaise
1 tablespoon snipped parsley
1 teaspoon chopped watercress
1 teaspoon chopped chives
1 teaspoon dill weed

Blend all the herbs into the mayonnaise. Chill until serving.

Mushroom Bourguignonne Sauce

1 small onion, finely chopped	1 1/2 cups BEEF STOCK
1 small carrot, finely chopped	1 tablespoon tomato
3 tablespoons oil	paste
3/4 cup sliced fresh mushrooms	1 teaspoon salt
2 tablespoons flour	pepper to taste
1/4 cup red wine	1 bay leaf

Sauté the onion and carrot, in oil, until onion is golden. Stir in mushrooms and flour; cook until brown. Add remaining ingredients. Bring the sauce to a boil, and simmer uncovered for 30 minutes. Remove from heat and take the bay leaf out of the sauce.

Fire up your fondue pot for a special gathering with close friends. Try one or all of our seasoned sauces to accompany the beef.

Pacific Flank Steak

Marinade:
3/4 cup oil
1/4 cup soy sauce
3 tablespoons honey
2 tablespoons red wine
    vinegar

1 clove garlic
1 1/2 teaspoons ground
    ginger
1 green onion, chopped

2 pounds flank steak,
    sliced thin

. . . simply delicious.

In a small bowl combine all marinade ingredients and mix well. Place steak in a large plastic bag, pour marinade over and secure bag tightly. Allow meat to marinate in refrigerator for at least five hours, turning several times.

Grill about 2 inches above "white hot" coals or under broiler for 4 to 5 minutes on each side. To serve, slice thin strips diagonally across the grain of the meat.

6 servings

Baked Ham basted with Rum

4 pounds ham
2 oranges, unpeeled
1 cup dark rum

1 tablespoon whole cloves
2 tablespoons mustard
1/2 cup brown sugar

This ham takes about 4 hours to bake. The orange slices in the marinade are almost as delicious as the ham.

Preheat oven to 300°.

Line roasting pan with foil. Place ham in pan and cover with an additional piece of foil. Bake at 300° for 2 hours. Remove ham from oven. Take ham and foil out of the pan and line bottom of pan with clean foil.

Slice oranges and line the foil with them. Pour rum over the oranges. Remove fat and hide from ham. Score in a pleasing pattern. Push cloves into meat, evenly spaced. Replace ham in roasting pan and cover with foil. Bake at 300° for 1 hour, basting often with rum.

Mix mustard and brown sugar together. Remove foil from ham and gently spread mustard mixture over the top of ham. Bake for 1 more hour, uncovered.

8-10 servings

Pork Chops
with Red Apples

2 tablespoons oil

2 medium red cooking apples, cored and cut into
    thick slices

4 to 6 pork loin chops

2 green onions, chopped

1 teaspoon salt

1/8 teaspoon pepper

1 1/2 cups apple juice

1 tablespoon cornstarch

1/4 cup heavy cream

parsley sprigs for garnish

Heat oil in an electric frying pan or heavy skillet over medium
heat. Cook apples for 5 minutes or until tender, turning slices
once. Remove apple slices to a warm serving dish.

Add chops to oil in skillet and cook over medium high heat
until browned, about 10 minutes. Add onions, salt, pepper,
and 1 1/4 cups apple juice. Bring to a boil and reduce heat to
low. Cover and simmer 10 minutes or until meat is fork tender.
Remove chops to warm platter.

In a small bowl, blend cornstarch and remaining 1/4 cup apple
juice until smooth. Gradually stir into skillet. Add cream and
cook stirring constantly until mixture is slightly thickened.
Pour sauce over pork chops and apples and garnish with
parsley.

4 servings

Whidbey's warm autumn
days and clear crisp nights help
make local apples especially
juicy and sweet. Liz Kline
couples pork chops with apples
for a superb flavor combination.

*In 1929 Whidbey Island
Indians hosted Coupeville's Indian
Water Festival. Indians visited
from all over the state and took
part in log rolling, tree falling,
a fisherman's race, and
International War Canoe Races.*

Lamb Curry with Fruit

2 pounds lean boneless lamb
1 tablespoon oil
1 large onion, chopped
2 cloves garlic, pressed
3 teaspoons curry powder
1 teaspoon ginger
1 cup apple juice
1 cup BEEF STOCK
1 tablespoon cornstarch
4 nectarines
4 cups cooked rice

Condiments: coconut chips
              chutney
              salted peanuts, chopped
              hard boiled eggs, chopped

Cut lamb into 1-inch cubes and sprinkle with salt and pepper. Brown meat in a skillet over medium heat until the meat is brown on all sides. Set aside.

Add onion, garlic, curry and ginger to skillet and cook until onion is tender. Stir in apple juice and beef stock, scraping browned particles free from pan.

Return meat to pan and bring to a boil. Cover, reduce heat and simmer for 1 hour. Skim and discard fat.

In a small bowl combine cornstarch and 1 tablespoon water. Add to the pan and cook over medium heat, stirring until sauce thickens. Add nectarines and cook until heated through.

Pass Lamb Curry to be served over individual servings of hot rice. Condiments are sprinkled over curry to suit the individual taste.

8 servings

The distinct flavor of lamb is enhanced with the addition of nectarines in this easy to serve entrée. Peggy Moore serves Lamb Curry over boiled rice with a selection of condiments.

Curry continues to be a very popular flavoring in Britain, a legacy of old colonial times. Always stir curries with a wooden spoon.

Stuffed Leg of Lamb

1 tablespoon butter

1/2 onion, chopped

3 cloves garlic

1/2 cup bread crumbs

1 1/2 teaspoons fresh rosemary

1/3 teaspoon fresh ginger

1/3 teaspoon pepper

1/2 cup chopped parsley

1 1/2 teaspoons anchovy paste

3 pound leg of lamb, boned and butterflied

1 tablespoon oil

1 tablespoon soy sauce

We prefer to have the butcher bone and butterfly our lamb. If that is not possible, there are many reference books in print which describe the technique of boning various types of meat.

Preheat oven to 450°.

To prepare stuffing, melt butter in large skillet. Soften onion and garlic in butter over medium heat. Add bread crumbs, rosemary, ginger, pepper, parsley and anchovy paste. Mix well.

Spread the leg of lamb flat so that the meat is the same thickness all across. Spread stuffing mixture over the meat, roll it and tie with twine to secure a neat bundle.

Stir oil and soy sauce together. Sprinkle the stuffed lamb with the oil and soy sauce mixture.

Reduce oven temperature to 350°. Bake the leg of lamb at 350° for 90 minutes or until the meat thermometer reaches 175° for medium rare meat.

6 servings

Lyn Murphy perks up lamb roast with the spicy addition of fresh ginger and rosemary in the dressing. Sprinkle the lamb with oil and soy sauce before baking the meat.

If you are lucky enough to have leftover stuffed lamb, place very thin slices of cold meat on sliced baguettes with a pinch of Dijon mustard. Delicious!

A View of the Olympic Mountains

Langley Winter Mystery Weekend Late Night Repast

Langley, on South Whidbey Island, is a small seaside village that has retained its colorful culture and natural beauty. Some say Langley has a "timelessness" about it. Langley residents love a cause for celebration and each February they celebrate in style. Langley hosts Mystery Weekend providing participants an opportunity to solve a bogus murder using crime synopsis, map and clues picked up in the shops of town.

Continental Cheese Fondue with Sourdough Cubes and Fruit

Smoked Salmon Antipasto

Strawberries Devonshire

Boudoir Cheesecake

Whidbeys Hot Chocolate Decadence

Deception Pass State Park Afternoon Barbeque

Deception Pass State Park is located on the west side of Whidbey Island's north end. The park is the busiest of all the state's parks. It contains 3,000 acres of old forestland, 251 campsites, 306 picnic sites, 17 miles of beachfront property, 20 miles of forest trails and three freshwater lakes. Visitors are offered a host of recreational activities including fantastic bird watching. The most distinctive attraction is the breathtaking view from Deception Pass Bridge connecting Whidbey Island to Fidalgo Island. For more information about Deception Pass State Park visit the Interpretive Museum at the park which chronicles the life of the Civilian Conservation Corps that constructed the park in the mid-1930s.

Vegetable Cheese Spread with Crackers

Barbequed Salmon in Citrus and Wine

Peg's Pasta Salad

Tarragon Asparagus

Four Seed Crunchy Bread

Washington Apple Cake

King Salmon with Onion Marmalade and Whidbey Port Sauce

8 salmon medallions,
   3 ounces each

3 onions, diced small

2 cups fish stock

1 tablespoon white wine
   vinegar

salt and pepper from
   the mill

2 cups heavy cream

4 tablespoons flour

2 tablespoons peanut oil

2 cloves shallots,
   minced

2 ounces mushrooms,
   sliced

1/4 cup Whidbeys Port

1 cup sweet butter

Create a stunning impression when you serve this dramatic entrée sent to us by Paul Divina of the *Star Bistro* in Langley.

To prepare marmalade, place the onions, 1 cup of the fish stock and vinegar in a skillet; season with salt and pepper. Cover and cook over medium heat 12 to 15 minutes or until the liquid has evaporated. Set aside and keep warm.

Over medium heat, reduce 1 cup of the cream by 3/4 of a cup. Fold into the onion mixture.

Season the salmon with salt and pepper; dredge in flour and quickly sauté in the oil until not quite done. Remove the medallions to a warm plate and cover to keep warm.

To prepare the port sauce, pour the excess oil from the skillet and add the shallots and mushrooms. Deglaze with the port and remaining 1 cup fish stock. Reduce to about 1/4 cup. Add the remaining 1 cup cream and stir until the mixture is reduced and thickened. Remove from the heat and with a swirling motion add the butter (a little at a time) until it is fully incorporated. Strain the port sauce through a fine sieve, pressing all of the liquid out of the shallot mushroom mixture.

To serve, divide the marmalade among 4 heated plates, place 2 medallions on the marmalade and top with the sauce.

4 servings

Barbequed Salmon in Citrus and Wine

4-5 pounds whole salmon fillet
1/2 pound butter
1 lemon
1 orange
1 medium onion
1 cup sherry wine
1/2 teaspoon salt
lemon, sliced for garnish

Light charcoal 35 to 40 minutes before you plan to begin cooking. Skin and remove bones from salmon.

Cut the butter into small pieces and spread on the bottom of a flat metal baking pan. Slice lemon and orange into 1/4 inch thick rounds and spread over butter. Slice onion to 1/4 inch thickness and spread over citrus. Pour wine over all.

Lay salmon fillet in pan on top of other ingredients. Sprinkle with salt.

When coals are covered with grey ash arrange them in a single layer. Place pan with fish on grill over charcoal. Close cover and open dampers just enough to maintain moderate heat and contain smoke in cooker to flavor salmon.

Lift grill cover and baste with sauce from under salmon every 5 minutes until salmon is cooked through (about 20 minutes). Fish will flake apart when prodded gently with a fork in its thickest part.

Place salmon on a warm platter and surround with the lemon slices.

8 servings

Enjoy casual elegance at the *Blueberry Hill Restaurant* while dining on barbequed salmon served in citrus and wine. We are pleased to be able to offer *Blueberry Hill's* recipe for this house specialty.

Chinook salmon is also commonly known as king, tyee, blackmouth or spring salmon. Although it is the least abundant species it is a very important sport and commercial fish.

White King Salmon with Sun Dried Tomato, Leeks and Cream

4 (8 ounce) fillet portions of white king salmon
1 pound butter
1 cup plus 1 tablespoon flour
3 cups fish stock
1.5 litre white wine
3 ounces dried tomato
2 spring cut leeks
1 cup cream
salt and white pepper to taste

Remove pin bones from each fillet.

Melt butter in the top of a double boiler. Separate and dispose of the milk solids from the butter. Remove and heat 3 ounces of the butter in a heavy pan.

Preheat oven to 375°.

Add the flour to the butter and cook over low heat for 5 minutes. While this is happening, heat the stock with 1 cup of wine to boiling. Temper the flour and butter mixture with 1 cup of the wine stock. Add remaining stock mixture to the flour and butter mixture. Cook over medium heat until it is reduced by 1/3.

Cut the tomato into thin strips and add to the stock as it reduces. Wash and dice leeks into quarter inch pieces, draining well. Once stock has reduced, add leeks to the mixture with 1 cup cream. Season with salt and pepper and hold sauce over low heat.

In a baking pan, place the salmon skin-side-down and cover each piece of fish with 1 tablespoon butter. Cover bottom of the pan with the remaining white wine. Bake salmon at 375° for 10 minutes per inch of thickness of the fillet. Do not overcook.

Remove fish from pan, sauce immediately, and serve quickly.

4 servings

The heart of the *Inn at Langley* is its country kitchen, where guests and local residents gather to sample an exceptional display of intriguing Northwest dishes. Several nights a week Stephen Nogal prepares a prix fixe supper from local ingredients, some of which are grown in the Inn's own garden.

The leek has been called "The Poor Man's Asparagus."

Salmon Patties

1 1/2 tablespoons butter

4 tablespoons Minute Tapioca

1 tablespoon minced onion

1 teaspoon chopped parsley

1/2 teaspoon vinegar

dash of salt and pepper

3/4 cup milk

1 cup salmon, cooked and flaked

1 cup fine bread crumbs

2 tablespoons oil

Garnish: parsley
          lemon quarters

Combine all ingredients. Be sure they are well mixed. Form into patties about 2 inches in diameter.

Brown patties in oil over medium heat. Remove them and place on a serving plate.

Garnish salmon patties with parsley and lemon quarters and serve hot.

4 servings

When Freida Weaver has an abundance of cooked salmon she makes some of it into Salmon Patties.

Meerkerk Rhododendron Gardens are located in the central Whidbey area. The gardens contain 1,500 species of gorgeous Rhododendrons growing on 53 acres of land. This land was willed to the Seattle Rhododendron Society by Ann Meerkerk for preservation. The gardens are open to visitors when the flowers are at their peak time for blooming, during April and May.

King Salmon in Champagne Sauce with Penn Cove Mussels

1 tablespoon butter
3 medium shallots, peeled and
    sliced
2 medium mushrooms, sliced
2/3 cup brut champagne
24 fresh mussels in shell, beard
    removed and rinsed

2/3 cup crème fraîche (see below)
10 teaspoons cold sweet butter, cut
    into 1-teaspoon size pieces
4 (6 ounce) salmon fillets

salt and pepper to taste

Preheat oven to 400°.

In a large saucepan melt butter. Add shallots and mushrooms and
sauté until soft. Add champagne and mussels. Watch carefully as the
sauce will be extremely foamy at first due to the champagne. The
mussels should steam open within a few minutes. When all mussels
have opened, remove them with a slotted spoon. Place in a covered
dish and set aside.

Over moderate heat reduce liquid in pan to 1/2 cup. Whisk crème
fraîche into reduced liquid and bring to a boil. Remove from heat and
whisk in 8 teaspoons of sweet butter a few pieces at a time until all
butter has been incorporated. Set aside in a warm place.

Place salmon in an ovenproof pan. Add 1/4 cup water and dot each
piece with 1/2 teaspoon sweet butter. Lightly season fillets with salt
and pepper. Bake in a 400° oven for 6 to 8 minutes. Since salmon is so
easy to overcook, watch it carefully during the cooking process.

Reheat sauce gently, whisking constantly and season to taste with salt
and pepper. To serve, strain sauce and ladle onto 4 heated plates. Place
salmon in center and 3 mussels on each side.

Crème Fraîche

1 cup heavy cream
1/2 cup sour cream or 2 teaspoons buttermilk

Combine heavy cream and sour cream or buttermilk. Stir the mixture
over low heat until just lukewarm. Pour into a clean jar and let sit at
room temperature until set (overnight should do). Cover and keep
refrigerated for up to one week.

4 servings

Above the Star Store in
Langley, Chef Paul Divina
prepares innovative cuisine with
fresh local ingredients. The *Star
Bistro* is a popular lunch and
dinner spot for the residents of
Langley as well as visitors.

*Crème fraîche is a naturally
fermented cream used in the
preparation of many French
dishes. It is available in some
specialty food stores. A suitable
substitute can be made at home.*

Race Lagoon Mussels with Corn and Red Pepper Sauce

2 pounds fresh mussels
4 tablespoons butter
1 cup white wine
4 cups CHICKEN STOCK
1/2 cup flour
2 large red peppers
1 small bunch parsley
1 pound fresh or frozen corn kernels
1 1/2 cups cream
salt and white pepper
1/4 cup + 1 tablespoon peanut oil

Clean mussels and remove beards. Cover with a damp cloth.

In a heavy pan melt butter over medium heat. In a second pan bring wine and chicken stock to a boil. Add flour to melted butter and reduce heat to low. Stir the flour and butter roux until it begins to brown. Add 1 cup of the wine and stock mixture and cook over low heat until volume is reduced by one third.

Dice red pepper into 1/4 inch chunks. Chop parsley. Purée corn in food processor until smooth. Add cream, corn purée, red pepper, and parsley to sauce. Season to taste with salt and pepper. Hold sauce warm until ready to use.

In a heavy pan or wok heat peanut oil. Add mussels and coat evenly with oil. Cover with a lid, cooking until shells begin to open. Pour sauce over the mussels and stir well to coat all mussels.

Evenly distribute the mussels into 4 warm bowls and serve immediately.

4 servings

The *Inn at Langley* offers 24 rooms overlooking Saratoga Passage. Guests are pampered with European comforters, whirlpool tubs, private porches and wood burning fireplaces in each room. Innkeeper and Chef, Stephen Nogal, and his staff host conferences and welcome guests to the quiet pace of island life. Several times each week Stephen creates haute cuisine designed to delight the eye as well as the palate.

Penn Cove Mussels, which began in 1975, is the oldest and largest mussel farm in the country. It is owned by Ian and Rawl Jefferds. Penn Cove Mussels rakes in around 1/2 million pounds of mussels a year. They are distributed to markets in Seattle and around the world within 24 hours of the harvest.

Stuffed Penn Cove Mussels

1 pound Penn Cove Mussels (approximately 25 to 30)

2 cloves garlic

2 tablespoons minced onion

1 tablespoon currants

1 tablespoon chopped fresh parsley

1 1/2 teaspoons dill weed

1/2 teaspoon tarragon

1/2 cup cooked rice

1 1/2 cups bread crumbs

1 tablespoon lemon juice

1/2 cup white wine or seafood stock

1/4 cup Parmesan cheese

2 tablespoons melted butter

This recipe presents yet another delicious way to serve Penn Cove Mussels. This local favorite was contributed by Christopher Panek, owner/chef of *Christopher's* restaurant in Coupeville.

Clean and "debeard" mussels. After debearding the mussels, open them by inserting a knife into the spot where the beard was before it was removed. Slide the knife toward the wide end of the mussel shell and pop the shell open. Remove the top shell and set aside.

To prepare the stuffing, combine all remaining ingredients in an electric blender or food processor. Spin until well blended.

Preheat oven to 425°.

Spoon 1 tablespoon stuffing over each mussel in shell. Place the mussels on a baking sheet and bake at 425° for 10 minutes.

Serve immediately.

4 servings

A portion of the success in any mussel recipe depends on proper cleansing before they are prepared. Mussels should be washed in very cold water. All attached shells and barnacles should be scraped from the shells. To remove the stringy, black beard protruding from the shell, grasp tightly with pliers and pull towards the large rounded end of the shell. Place mussels in a bowl covered with ice cubes until you are ready to prepare them.

Stuffed Olympic Oysters

2 dozen oysters on the half shell
9 cups rock salt

1 cup chopped green onion
1/4 cup minced parsley
6 cloves garlic, minced
1/4 cup butter
1/2 cup flour
2 cups half and half
1/4 cup sherry
1 teaspoon salt
1 teaspoon freshly ground pepper

1/2 teaspoon cayenne
4 egg yolks, beaten
1/2 cup chopped mushrooms
1/2 pound cooked shrimp,
    diced

Topping:
6 tablespoons freshly grated
    Parmesan cheese
4 tablespoons bread crumbs
1/2 teaspoon paprika
1/2 teaspoon salt

. . . the ultimate opportunity to indulge.

To prepare oysters, wash and dry the shells. Spread 3 cups rock salt on each of three baking sheets.

Early in the day, cook green onions, parsley and garlic in butter over low heat for 10 minutes, stirring constantly. Add flour a little at a time. Add half and half, stirring until mixture is smooth. Add sherry, salt, pepper and cayenne.

Stir in egg yolks and cook over low heat until mixture thickens. Stir in mushrooms and cook for 2 minutes over low heat. Add shrimp and continue cooking for 3 minutes. At this time the sauce should be quite thick. Pour sauce into a glass bowl and allow to cool at room temperature. Cover with plastic wrap and refrigerate for at least 1 1/2 hours.

To prepare topping, blend all ingredients in an electric blender on high speed.

Preheat oven to 500° at least 45 minutes before you plan to serve the oysters. Place trays of rock salt in oven while it is preheating.

Put an oyster on each shell and place 8 shells on each hot tray of rock salt. Spoon 1 1/2 tablespoons of shrimp sauce over each oyster. Sprinkle each oyster with 1 teaspoon topping mixture. Bake at 500° for 15 minutes. Oysters should be well browned on top.

6 servings

Scampi

18-20 large, raw shrimp, shelled and deveined
2 tablespoons olive oil
2 tablespoons butter
2 cloves garlic, minced
dash Italian seasoning
2 tablespoons chopped parsley
2 tablespoons seasoned dry bread crumbs
2 tablespoons grated Parmesan cheese

Clean shrimp and store in refrigerator until just before serving.

Preheat broiler.

Heat oil in a large heavy ovenproof skillet; add butter, garlic and Italian seasoning. Add shrimp and sauté until almost done, about 3 minutes.

Sprinkle shrimp with parsley, bread crumbs and cheese. Place scampi under broiler for 30 seconds, just long enough for cheese to bubble slightly.

Serve immediately.

4 servings

For a special occasion Jim Seabolt suggests serving Scampi. Ste. Michelle Johannisberg Riesling wine would nicely complement this light seafood dish.

The birds of Whidbey Island are on display each season of the year. Whidbey is home to the grand bald eagle, great blue heron, and many species of the loon, hawk, duck, and others. The Whidbey Audubon Society is very active and they keep a yearly count of individual birds belonging to 113 species.

Dungeness Crab with Butters and Lemon Mayonnaise Sauce

This method of cleaning crab is preferable to cooking crab whole because the meat does not become contaminated with the entrails when cooked.

Clean the crab right after it is caught. Kill the crab with a swift blow between the eyes. Grab the top of the shell on each side and place your thumbs in the middle of the shell. Pull the shell inward causing it to break in half. Pull the shell off the crab. Clean out the center section of the crab which contains the entrails. Rinse under very cold water. Boil the crab for 15 minutes. The crab will be bright orange. Remove crab from boiling water and rinse with very cold water. This loosens the meat in the shell and makes the crab easy to crack. If you are not eating the crab immediately, place the crab in a bowl and cover it with ice. Refrigerate until serving.

Lemon Mayonnaise

In a blender or a food processor, whirl 2 egg yolks, 1 1/2 tablespoons lemon juice and 1 teaspoon grated lemon peel. Slowly add 1 cup olive oil. This may be refrigerated for 2 days.

To prepare the following butters, place all ingredients in a small saucepan. Heat the butter until it has melted and add the additional ingredients. Serve warm.

Anchovy Butter

3 tablespoons butter
1 tablespoon anchovy oil
2 tablespoons minced anchovy fillets
1 tablespoon fresh lemon juice

Lemon and Caper Butter

1/4 cup butter
2 tablespoons capers
1 tablespoon fresh lemon juice

Onion Butter

1/4 cup butter
1/2 cup minced onion

Soy Sauce Butter

3 tablespoons butter
3 tablespoons soy sauce

4 servings each

One of the rewards of living on Whidbey Island is the opportunity to catch fresh Dungeness crab. We have several spots where we catch crab that are large and deep red. Dungeness seems to be the most flavorful and meaty crab of all the varieties.

We suggest serving the cooked crab with a choice of the butters and sauce below. They are simple to prepare and they each complement the crab nicely. Be sure to offer fresh baguettes and a dry Sauvignon Blanc wine or a mellow Ste. Michelle Merlot.

Crab and Shrimp Sandwich

1 pound cream cheese, at room temperature

1/2 pound fresh crabmeat

1/2 pound small shrimp

2 tablespoons chives, chopped

juice of 1/2 lemon

2 dashes tabasco

1 dash worcestershire

1/4 teaspoon white pepper

8 slices sourdough bread

8 slices cheddar cheese

Mix all ingredients except bread and cheddar cheese together in an electric mixer.

Divide evenly among bread slices and spread to cover bread. Place sandwiches on a broiler pan. Top each with a slice of cheese and cook under broiler until cheese is melted and begins to bubble.

Garnish as suggested above or to suit your own taste and serve immediately.

8 servings

This open faced sandwich was created for the *Captain Whidbey Inn* by Chef Lorren W. Garlichs. At the Inn individual servings are garnished with fresh asparagus spears, hard boiled eggs, sliced black olives, pickles, tomatoes, and a lemon wedge.

Located on the south side of Langley, Whidbey Island Vineyard is flourishing under the tender care of Greg and Elizabeth Osenbach. They have developed an off dry, slightly fruity blend of wine from a combination of three white European grapes. According to Elizabeth this wine is a "drinkable" wine and can be enjoyed with an afternoon snack, an evening meal or by itself. We suggest you try "Siegerrebe" with the Captain Whidbey Crab and Shrimp Sandwich.

Crab Broccoli Bake

1 1/2 pounds broccoli
1/3 cup chopped almonds
1/4 cup butter
3 tablespoons flour
1/2 teaspoon salt
1/8 teaspoon pepper
1 chicken bouillon cube
1 1/2 cups milk
1 tablespoon lemon juice
12 ounces fresh crab meat
2 tablespoons grated Parmesan cheese

Preheat oven to 400°.

Plunge broccoli into salted boiling water. Allow broccoli to cook 1 minute and drain. Arrange broccoli in a shallow 2-quart baking dish.

In a small skillet lightly brown almonds in 1 tablespoon butter over medium heat. Remove from the heat and set aside.

Melt remaining butter in a small pan over medium heat. Whisk in flour, salt, pepper, and crushed bouillon cube. Gradually stir in milk. Cook, stirring constantly, until the sauce has thickened. Remove the sauce from the heat and stir in lemon juice. Fold in crab meat.

Spoon crab and sauce over broccoli. Sprinkle with toasted almonds and cheese. Bake at 400° for 15 minutes.

Serve immediately.

4 servings

Enjoy the delicate flavor of crab enhanced with a light cream sauce and fresh broccoli.

"The ornament of the house is the guests who frequent it."

– Anonymous

Scallops Cotswold

1 pound scallops
BOUQUET GARNI, or
   1 bay leaf, 2 sprigs parsley
   and 1/2 teaspoon tarragon
1/2 cup white wine
3 tablespoons butter
juice from 1/2 lemon
1/4 pound fresh mushrooms,
   sliced
1/2 cup finely chopped onion

2 tablespoons flour
1 egg yolk, beaten
2 tablespoons heavy cream

Garnish:
1/2 cup fine dry bread
   crumbs
1/2 cup grated Swiss cheese
1/4 cup snipped parsley

For a marvelous and impressive main course, serve Joan Norman's entrée, Scallops Cotswold.

The scallops, mushrooms and onions are prepared in a cream sauce which complements their flavors. Serve the scallop dish with a leafy green salad and plenty of freshly baked bread.

In a saucepan, cover the rinsed scallops with cold water (about 2 cups). Place the packet of bouquet garni in the water with the scallops. If you are using loose herbs, place them in the water at this time. Bring the water to a boil. Add the white wine and simmer for 10 minutes. Remove the bouquet garni, or the bay leaf and parsley. Remove the scallops with a slotted spoon, to a warm baking dish, reserving all liquid.

In a skillet melt 1 tablespoon butter over medium heat. Add the lemon juice to the butter. Sauté the mushrooms and onion in the skillet for 10 minutes. With a slotted spatula remove the mushrooms and onions from the skillet and place them with the scallops.

In the same skillet, melt the remaining 2 tablespoons butter. Stir in the flour and add the reserved liquid from the scallops. Stir until smooth. Thicken the sauce with the egg yolk and cream, stirring constantly (about 5 minutes).

Pour sauce over the scallops, mushrooms and onions. Mix all together. At this time the scallop mixture can be divided among 4 individual baking dishes or placed in a 2-quart baking dish. Cover the scallop mixture with the bread crumbs, cheese and parsley.

Bake in a 375° oven for 15 minutes. Serve immediately.

4 servings

Seafood Pasta

1/2 pound scallops

1/2 pound medium size prawns

1/2 pound fresh crab meat

2 shallots, chopped

1 tablespoon fresh parsley, chopped

1/2 teaspoon tarragon

salt and pepper to taste

2 tablespoons olive oil

1/4 cup dry Vermouth

1 pound fresh pasta

Preheat oven to 400°.

Combine scallops, prawns and cooked crab meat in an ovenproof casserole. Sprinkle with shallots, parsley and tarragon. Season to taste with salt and pepper. Drizzle olive oil and Vermouth over all.

Bake at 400° for 10 minutes.

While seafood is baking bring 2 quarts of salted water to a boil. Add fresh pasta to boiling water and cook for 2 or 3 minutes. Rinse quickly with cold water and then again with hot water. Allow to drain.

Divide pasta among 4 warm plates and spoon seafood over. Serve immediately.

4 servings

We are lucky enough to have friends that scuba dive in the area and provide us with the bounties of Puget Sound. We like to bake their catch and serve it over fresh pasta.

Puget Sound is rich with nutrients, creating a marine area which houses octopi up to 15 feet and long slinky wolf eels.

Keystone Underwater Park on Central Whidbey provides an aquatic park where divers can see a wealth of invertebrate life. Giant barnacles, scallops and flowery sea anemones float through the water. The winter months provide better visibility for divers because plankton that thrive on sunlight disappear during the dark winter months.

Whidbey Fish Chowder

Amounts according to tastes

Ingredients:

    potatoes

    carrots

    celery

    corn

    geoduck or butter clams

    halibut or cod

    prawns

    1/2 or cream

    pepper, thyme, dill

To a large pot of water - add thyme, dill & pepper - bring to boil.

Add, sequentially, potatoes, celery & carrots so that each is cooked but still a tad crunchy.

Steam halibut or cod bones in separate pot - add stock and picked fish to vegetable pot.

Sauté sliced geoduck or butter clams, boil and peel prawns and add to soup pot.

Sauté sliced green onions - add to pot.

Serve with cream or 1/2 & 1/2 - add ground pepper and shot of tabasco.

We anxiously awaited the arrival of the first recipe from a Whidbey Island establishment. Thom Gunn, owner of *Whidbey Fish Market and Café* in Greenbank, was prompt and we'd like to award Thom with the most unique presentation of a recipe. We're giving it to you just the way he gave it to us, but don't let the procedure keep you from trying this treat. *Whidbey Fish* Chowder is known at the Gunn household as "Jet Fuel."

Chowder is a gift from France. Fishermen in France made a communal stew from their catch at the end of the day. They cooked their fish stew in a heavy iron pot called a chaudière. Thus, the name of the stew became "chowder."

Bouillabaisse

4 tablespoons olive oil

2 leeks, chopped

1 large onion, chopped

1 stalk celery, chopped

salt and pepper to taste

1/2 teaspoon saffron

12 large prawns

18 sea scallops

24 mussels

2 pounds halibut

2 pounds red snapper

1 cup white wine

1 (12 ounce) can clam juice

2 large tomatoes, peeled and chopped

In a large kettle, heat the olive oil and sauté the leeks, onion and celery for 1 minute.

Add the seasonings to the vegetables. Place all shellfish and fish in the kettle and blend together.

Add the wine, clam juice and tomatoes to the kettle and cook for 10 minutes over medium high heat.

To serve Bouillabaisse divide the shellfish and fish into 6 soup bowls. Ladle the bouillon over the fish. Accompany with French bread and a salad.

6 servings

The Franssen family own and operate the *Kasteel Franssen*, a charming restaurant located in Oak Harbor. Bouillabaisse at *Kasteel Franssen* includes prawns, scallops, mussels, halibut and red snapper in a rich tomato stock. Mike Franssen suggests that the bouillabaisse be served in large bowls with slices of crusty French bread, and complemented by a Semillion Blanc wine.

Bouillabaisse is a traditional fish stew from southern France. The recipe actually originated with the Romans. Roman and French cooks made the stew with fish unique to the Mediterranean. They added saffron, herbs and olive oil to the fish such as racasse, rouquier and girelle. This traditional dish has been passed along from generation to generation.

Barbequed Halibut

2 pounds halibut fillet
1/2 cup butter
juice of 1 lemon
1 teaspoon dill
1 teaspoon pepper
2 cloves garlic, minced
1 tablespoon chopped fresh parsley

Pat halibut dry between two paper towels.

Melt butter and stir in lemon juice, dill, pepper, minced garlic and parsley.

Wrap fillet and butter mixture tightly in aluminum foil. Place on rack over hot coals and grill for 10 to 12 minutes, depending on the thickness of the fillet.

Spoon butter sauce over each serving.

6 servings

Whidbey Island anglers often reel in halibut from the waters of Deception Pass. If you believe their "fish stories," the fish can be as big as 100 pounds or more.

Patty Cohen likes the taste of grilled halibut with a well seasoned butter.

Sprinkle mesquite chips or apple branches on the coals to add more zest to your barbeque.

Halibut Dijon

1/2 cup oil
1 teaspoon salt
1 teaspoon pepper
2 cups flour
2 pounds halibut fillet
3 tablespoons butter
1 cup dry Vermouth
1/4 teaspoon nutmeg
1/8 teaspoon salt
1/8 teaspoon white pepper
1/4 cup Dijon mustard
1 cup heavy cream

Garnish: 1/2 lemon, sliced in thin rounds
           freshly chopped parsley

Heat oil in large pan over medium high heat. In a shallow dish mix salt, pepper and flour. Coat fish with flour mixture. Cook fish in oil until lightly browned on both sides, about 4 to 5 minutes. Fish is cooked when it flakes apart when gently prodded with a fork. Remove to serving dish and keep warm.

Melt butter in pan. Add Vermouth, nutmeg, salt, white pepper and mustard. Mix well with a wire whisk and bring to a boil. Add cream. Return to a boil and allow to boil rapidly until sauce thickens and is reduced to about 1 1/3 cups.

Pour sauce over halibut and garnish with lemon wheel slices.

Sprinkle lightly with freshly chopped parsley.

4 servings

Take advantage of every opportunity to purchase fresh halibut when available. At the *Blueberry Hill Restaurant*, Larry Reich serves halibut in a creamy Dijon sauce. Serve crisp vegetables to complement this entrée.

In 1853, North Whidbey property could be purchased for $1.25 per acre. Maylor's Point in Oak Harbor was purchased at such a price.

Pan Fried Smelt

3 pounds smelt
1/4 cup cornmeal
1/2 cup flour
1/2 teaspoon pepper
1 teaspoon salt
oil for frying
whole lemon

Clean smelt and wash thoroughly.

Combine cornmeal, flour, salt and pepper in a shallow dish. Dip smelt in water and then coat with the cornmeal mixture. Lay coated smelt on waxed paper and allow to set for 15 to 30 minutes.

Coat the bottom of a heavy skillet with oil. Fry smelt in hot oil for 4 minutes on each side. Smelt should be nicely browned. Drain on paper towels.

Serve with sliced lemon.

6 servings

When the smelt are running, Whidbey Islanders meet on the beach with fish nets and rakes to gather these small silver fish. Cleaning is a family affair and it seems each family has its own particular technique.

Irene Wanamaker, a native of Whidbey, offers her method of preparation.

Local Skagit Indians kept a watchful eye on the waters of Puget Sound. They were fearful of the hostile Haida Indians from the Queen Charlotte Islands in British Columbia. The Skagit Indians were forced to hide in order to escape death and enslavement when the Haidas landed on the shores of Whidbey Island from time to time.

Rolled Sole Fillets in Dill Sauce

2 pounds fillet of sole

black pepper and dill seed to taste

2 tablespoons butter

1 medium onion, sliced thin

2 carrots, peeled and cut into julienne strips

1 stalk celery, cut into julienne strips

1/2 cup white wine

1/2 cup CHICKEN STOCK

3 tablespoons butter

2 tablespoons flour

1/2 cup half and half

1 teaspoon Dijon mustard

Pat fillets dry with a paper towel and lay flat on sheets of waxed paper. Sprinkle with pepper and dill.

Sauté onion, carrots and celery in 2 tablespoons butter until tender. Place 1 to 2 tablespoons vegetables on each fillet. Roll each fillet around the vegetables and secure with a toothpick if necessary.

Arrange seam side down in a skillet and cover with wine and stock. Heat on high until bubbles form. Immediately reduce heat, cover and simmer 10 to 12 minutes. Remove fillets to a warm serving dish reserving 1 1/2 cups of liquid in the skillet. In a second pan, melt 3 tablespoons butter. Gradually stir in flour and continue stirring until flour is incorporated. Add stock mixture from skillet, cream and mustard. To suit individual tastes add more pepper and dill as needed.

Pour sauce over fillets of sole and serve immediately.

4 servings

The delicate flavor of sole is enhanced by julienned strips of vegetables. This is a favorite recipe from the kitchen of Sid Parker.

"The success of a dinner is readily judged by the manner in which conversation has been sustained."
– A. E. Davis, 1882

Ling Cod in Red Wine Sauce

1 1/2 pounds ling cod
salt and freshly ground pepper
1/4 cup flour
2 tablespoons olive oil
1 tablespoon butter
3/4 cup dry red wine
1 1/2 teaspoons butter
2 teaspoons chopped fresh parsley
1/2 lemon, cut in wedges
2 sprigs parsley

Season the ling cod with salt and pepper. Coat lightly with flour, shaking off the excess.

In a skillet, over medium heat, sauté the ling cod in hot oil and butter for 3 to 4 minutes per side, depending on the thickness of the fish. Remove fish from the skillet; transfer to a serving dish and keep warm.

Pour excess oil and butter from skillet. Deglaze skillet with wine. Add butter and parsley to the wine in the skillet and cook over medium heat until it is reduced by half.

Pour wine sauce over the ling cod and garnish with lemon wedges and parsley sprigs.

4 servings

Try fresh ling cod glazed in a mellow red wine sauce.

Lucky are those successful sport fishermen or friends of fishermen who are provided with fresh fish from local waters. Many others rely on obtaining their seafood from assorted markets.

When purchasing seafood turn down any that is "fishy smelling." A whole fish should have bright eyes, red gills and shiny moist skin. Fillets should appear to be moist and tight grained.

When you reach home place the fish surrounded in ice, in the refrigerator, replacing melted ice as needed. Stored in this manner, fresh fish should keep for several days.

Trout with Almonds

4 trout, serving size
1 cup milk
2 tablespoons flour
4 tablespoons butter
1/2 cup sliced almonds
salt and pepper to taste
1 lemon, sliced for garnish

Dip trout in the milk and then in flour. Lay on waxed paper.

Melt butter in a large skillet over medium high heat. Put in trout and almonds. Season with salt and pepper. Cook trout for 7 minutes on each side. Remove trout to a warm platter. Shake the skillet well so that all the almonds are browned.

Garnish trout with browned almonds and lemon slices.

4 servings

Fresh water fishing on Whidbey Island is a popular sport. There are many small lakes on the island abundant with tasty fish such as trout and bass.

Northwest Red Snapper

2 pounds red snapper fillets
4 tablespoons butter
juice of 1 lemon
4 tablespoons white wine
1 red onion, sliced thin
1 large tomato, diced

Rinse snapper and pat dry. In a heavy skillet combine butter, lemon juice and wine. Over medium heat allow mixture to come to a boil. Add fillets and cover with onion slices and tomatoes. Reduce heat, cover and simmer for 5 minutes or until the fish flakes easily with a fork.

4 servings

Jane O'Kelley retains the sharp flavor of red snapper with this easy preparation.

Whidbey's Greenbank Farm and Loganberry Fields
Greenbank

Coupeville Arts and Crafts Dinner

The Coupeville Arts and Crafts Festival is held the second week of August each year. The little town of Coupeville is transformed from a sleepy waterfront village to a haven for thousands of visitors shopping for quality arts and crafts. A wine tasting art show begins the festivities on Friday night. Entertainment, food and arts are provided throughout the weekend with a portion of the proceeds funding civic projects. Visitors experience the unique sense of island magic that local residents appreciate.

Hot Artichoke Spread with Pita Chips

Stuffed Penn Cove Mussels

Orange Rice

Whidbey Spinach Salad

Island Blackberry Cobbler

Oak Harbor's Holland Happening Coffee Time

Holland Happening is an annual springtime celebration in Oak Harbor. The Dutch heritage and customs of many local residents is a predominant theme throughout the week. There are many activities that are part of the Holland Happening celebration. They include a popular Dutch dinner to which the public is invited, a grand parade complete with "Dutch Street Sweepers," a weekend arts fair and displays at the Holland gardens.

Sweetened Dutch Coffee

Olie Bollen

Jan Hagel

Dutch Roogerbred (Rye Bread) with Gouda Cheese

Almond Bars

Whidbey's Berry Pie

1/2 cup Whidbeys liqueur

1 1/4 cups sugar

5-8 tablespoons cornstarch (use more if using frozen berries)

3 cups raspberries

1 1/2 cups blackberries (if frozen, thaw and drain)

1 1/2 cups blueberries

1 cup boysenberries

1 double crust, unbaked pie shell

Preheat oven to 425°.

In a saucepan mix Whidbeys, sugar and cornstarch together and simmer over low heat until mixture begins to thicken. Remove from heat and mix in berries.

Place the filling in an unbaked pie shell. Dot filling with 2 tablespoons butter, cut up. Cover filling with top crust.

Bake pie at 425° for 25 minutes. Then, reduce heat to 350° and bake for 35 minutes.

8 servings

Whidbey's Greenbank Farm is a small winery which grows the most beautiful, plump loganberries in the Northwest. Located in the middle of the island, Whidbey's occupies property overlooking Holmes Harbor with Mt. Baker as a backdrop. The inviting red barn structure warmly welcomes visitors. Picnic by the pond, admire the lush loganberry fields, and sample the wines of Ste. Michelle and Whidbey's. M.W. Whidbey's has produced and bottled "Whidbeys Liqueur" using the fresh fruit flavor of local loganberries. The berries retain the brilliant color of raspberries with the tart juiciness of wild blackberries. The liqueur has become an instant classic and has been acclaimed as the world's best berry liqueur.

Whidbey's Farm also suggests serving vanilla ice cream with Whidbeys liqueur drizzled over the top. Or, try marinating fresh fruit pieces in Whidbeys for an hour before serving. As the folks at Whidbey's Greenbank Farm will tell you, the ideas for using Whidbeys liqueur are endless. "Uncork the possibilities!"

Fresh Berry Pies

Fresh Strawberry Pie

Betty McKenzie

4 cups fresh strawberries	1/4 teaspoon salt
1 baked pie shell	3 tablespoons cornstarch
1 cup sugar	1 tablespoon lemon juice

Wash and hull strawberries. Drain thoroughly.
Arrange 2 cups berries in the bottom of pie shell. Crush the remaining berries in a small saucepan and mix in sugar, salt and cornstarch. Cook this mixture, stirring constantly until it thickens. Remove from heat and stir in lemon juice. Allow the mixture to cool.

Spoon over berries in shell and chill until firm.

8 servings

Earn a reputation at home for serving Fresh Berry Pies. They are seasonal and simple. The recipes we have chosen are our favorites because the whole berries look spectacular nestled in the fresh fruit filling.

Fresh Raspberry Pie

4 cups fresh raspberries	3 tablespoons cornstarch
1 cup sugar	1 baked pie shell

Crush 1 cup berries in small saucepan and bring to a boil with 1 1/2 cups water. Lower heat and simmer for 3 minutes. Strain berries through a small mesh strainer or cheesecloth, reserving juice. Return juice to saucepan and add sugar and cornstarch. Boil for 3 minutes. Allow to cool.

Fill baked pie shell with 3 cups fresh berries. Pour the juice mixture over the berries and chill.

8 servings

Blueberry Cream Cheese Crepes

2 (3 ounce) packages cream cheese, at room temperature
1/4 cup sugar
1 teaspoon lemon juice
1/2 teaspoon vanilla
1 1/2 cups frozen blueberries
12 crepes
4 tablespoons butter, softened

In a small bowl, combine the cream cheese, sugar, lemon juice and vanilla until smooth and creamy. Fold in frozen blueberries.

Lay out the crepes on a flat surface. Spread 3 tablespoons of the cream cheese mixture in the center of each crepe. Fold each crepe over filling and roll into a tube shape.

Brush an ovenproof serving plate with 2 tablespoons of butter. Lay crepes on plate and brush the tops of crepes with remaining butter. Gently warm in a microwave or 300° oven.

Ladle Blueberry Sauce over crepes and enjoy.

Blueberry Sauce

4 tablespoons lemon juice
2 tablespoons cornstarch
3/4 cup sugar
2 cups blueberries

Mix 3/4 cup water with lemon juice and cornstarch until it is smooth. Add sugar and blueberries. Cook over high heat, stirring gently until the mixture begins to boil. Reduce heat to simmer and cook until thickened. Remove from heat.

Blueberry Sauce may be made ahead and stored in the refrigerator. Warm the sauce before serving over crepes.

12 crepes

Perched on a hill near Freeland, *Blueberry Hill* restaurant offers a panoramic view of Holmes Harbor. This establishment is renowned for its fine desserts prepared by owner and chef, Larry Reich.

Island Blackberry Cobbler

4-5 cups wild blackberries

3/4 cup sugar

1/2 cup margarine

1/8 teaspoon salt

1 cup flour

1 teaspoon baking powder

1/2 cup milk

1 cup sugar

1 tablespoon cornstarch

1 cup boiling water

Spread the berries evenly in a 9 x 13-inch baking dish. In a large mixing bowl cream together sugar and softened margarine. Add salt, flour and baking powder alternately with milk. Drop this batter by spoonfuls over the berries. Mix together 1 cup sugar and cornstarch and sprinkle over the batter. Pour boiling water evenly over all.

Bake at 375° for 45-60 minutes, or until top is light brown and berry juice is starting to set.

10 servings

We both have vivid childhood memories of spending hot summer afternoons searching through brambles for wild blackberries. Only the tiny variety would be suitable for Grandma's blackberry cobbler. Picking the berries was time consuming but worth every moment when we were finally treated to the taste of a freshly baked cobbler.

As a substitute for the blackberries, try using 4 cups rhubarb and 2 cups fresh sliced strawberries. Rhubarb grows prolifically in Whidbey soil. The tartness of young rhubarb set against the sweet crisp topping is an unbeatable combination. Serve the cobbler at room temperature.

Whidbeys Loganberry Champagne Spoom

1 cup sugar
4 egg whites
pinch of salt
1 quart LOGANBERRY
    SHERBET, softened

1 cup champagne
1/2 cup Whidbeys
    liqueur

In a heavy saucepan, heat sugar and 1/2 cup water to 238° on candy thermometer. Whip egg whites with a pinch of salt to form soft peaks.

Slowly add sugar mixture to egg whites in a small steady stream while whipping. Fold in softened sherbet to the above meringue.

Pour mixture into 12 stemmed glasses. Freeze until ready to serve. When ready to serve, top each with 1 tablespoon of Whidbeys liqueur, then with a splash of champagne.

12 servings

Loganberry Sherbet

10 ounces fresh
    loganberries
3/4 cup sugar
1 cup heavy cream

1 1/2 cups champagne
2 egg whites
1/2 teaspoon cream of
    tartar

Mash loganberries and set them aside. In a heavy pan, slowly heat 1/2 cup of the sugar and the cream until the sugar dissolves. Add loganberries and champagne. Freeze in an ice cream mixer, according to the manufacturer's directions, until almost firm.

Whip egg white, cream of tartar and 1/4 cup sugar to stiff peaks. Fold into the loganberry mixture and continue to freeze until firm.

6 servings

Whidbey Island's loganberries are the inspiration for two fine desserts created by Bill Davis.

Bill tops each serving of his "spoom" with a tablespoon of Whidbeys liqueur, then with a splash of champagne. The sherbet is sublime when served in tall, chilled parfait glasses.

Captain Whidbey Chocolate Ice Cream

4 cups heavy cream

8 egg yolks

1 cup sugar

2 teaspoons vanilla

6 ounces semi-sweet chocolate

8 ounces Whidbeys liqueur

Place 2 cups cream in the top of a large double boiler over hot water on moderate heat. Let stand, uncovered, until a slightly wrinkled skin forms on top of the cream.

Meanwhile beat the yolks for a few minutes until they are pale and thick. Gradually add the sugar and beat until a ribbon forms. Very gradually add half of the cream to the beaten yolks. Scrape the bowl well to mix. Add the yolk mixture and vanilla to the remaining cream. Mix well and place over hot water again, using moderate heat.

Cook the ingredients, while scraping the sides and bottom frequently, until the mixture thickens. It should register 180° on a candy thermometer. Remove from the water and transfer to a larger bowl.

Melt the chocolate in the liqueur until it can be whipped together without lumps. Add this to the hot cream mixture along with the remaining 2 cups of cream. Stir well and let cool. When completely cool, freeze in an ice cream machine, following the manufacturer's directions.

6 servings

Visitors at the *Captain Whidbey Inn* are in for an exciting and scenic treat as innkeeper, John Stone, offers the opportunity to sail the tranquil waters of Penn Cove aboard his sailboat. After sailing in the warm Whidbey sunshine, plunge into a rich dish of Captain Whidbey Chocolate Ice Cream.

Since it is only a few minutes from Langley, Whidbey Island Vineyard is easy to find and will prove well worth your time and effort. We learned that the actual process of making wine is not difficult, yet it is a task which requires the utmost attention to timing, nurturing and detail.

Greg and Elizabeth Osenbach have developed a "late harvest" wine; one to be savored as a sweet aperitif. It is a well bred, elegant wine that should be poured into cut crystal goblets and served ice cold.

Frozen Lemon Delight

3 eggs, separated
1/4 cup fresh lemon juice
rind of 1/2 lemon
1/8 teaspoon salt

1/2 cup plus 2 tablespoons sugar
1 cup heavy cream
1 cup crushed vanilla wafers
fresh lemon slices for garnish

Set aside egg whites. Beat yolks until lemon colored and combine with lemon juice, rind, salt and sugar. Cook, stirring constantly until thick. Allow to cool.

Beat egg whites until stiff. Whip cream and fold into egg whites. Add cooled custard.

Sprinkle 1/2 cup crushed wafers on the bottom of a loaf pan. Spread custard over wafers. Sprinkle remaining wafer crumbs on top. Freeze for at least four hours. Cut into slices to serve; garnish with a thinly sliced round of fresh lemon.

6 servings

Everyone appreciates a dessert that can be made ahead. Frozen Lemon Delight is served directly from the freezer and its subtle tang is a welcome end to a fine meal.

Amaretto Alarms

1/2 gallon vanilla ice cream
1 egg
1 teaspoon vanilla
1/3 cup Amaretto liqueur
1/2 cup chocolate syrup
1/2 cup milk, or as much as needed for desired consistency
slivered almonds for garnish

Combine all ingredients together in an electric blender. Mix until they are smooth and creamy. Serve in individual stemware with garnish.

6 servings

Julie Wilson never sends her guests home feeling hungry after topping a light entrée with her Amaretto chocolate concoction. It is similar to a milk shake in consistency and looks lovely served in tall stemware. Julie garnishes each serving with swirls of chocolate sauce and slivered almonds.

Meringue Lemon Dessert

Meringue:

6 egg whites

1/4 teaspoon cream of tartar

1 teaspoon lemon juice

1 1/2 cups sugar

Filling:

6 egg yolks

the juice and grated rind of one lemon

dash of salt

3/4 cup sugar

2 cups heavy cream, whipped

Preheat oven to 250°.

In a large mixing bowl, beat the egg whites until frothy. Add the cream of tartar and lemon juice and mix well. While mixing, add the sugar gradually. Beat until the sugar has dissolved and stiff peaks begin to form. Spread meringue in a buttered 9 x 13-inch pan. Bake 45 minutes at 250°. Turn off the oven heat and leave the meringue in the oven overnight, or for a minimum of 5 hours.

To prepare the filling, beat the egg yolks in a large mixing bowl until they are thick and lemon yellow in color. Add the lemon juice and rind, salt and sugar to the yolks. Transfer this mixture into the top of a double boiler and stir until the mixture coats the spoon. Cool.

To assemble the dessert, spread half of the whipped cream over the meringue. Top with all of the lemon filling mixture. Cover with remaining whipped cream.

Store the dessert in the refrigerator and garnish each individual serving with lemon twists.

12 servings

Jeanne Skinner enjoys making this dessert because of its versatility. It is delightful at her office staff luncheons and it is light enough to be served in the evening as well. Jeanne prepares Meringue Lemon Dessert the night before so it can chill in the refrigerator.

Berry Rhubarb Fool

3/4 pound (about 3 cups) rhubarb, sliced into
    1-inch pieces
1/2 cup sugar
1/4 cup orange juice
dash of salt
3/4 cup heavy cream, whipped
3 cups strawberries, quartered
6 whole strawberries for garnish

In a medium saucepan combine rhubarb, sugar, orange juice and salt. Cover and simmer 7 minutes or until rhubarb is tender. Cool slightly. Pour rhubarb mixture into a blender. Cover and blend until it is smooth, then chill the mixture.

Just before serving, slightly fold whipped cream and 2 cups strawberries into rhubarb mixture. The rhubarb should look streaked with the colors of berries and cream.

In 6 chilled parfait glasses, layer rhubarb berry mixture with the remaining cup of sliced strawberries. Garnish each parfait with a whole strawberry.

6 servings

Mick and Christy Heggenes are eager to welcome guests at their Bed and Breakfast which is aptly named, *Christy's Country Inn*. After a day of island exploration, retreat to the warmth and charm of this lovely country style home. Lounge on the spacious private deck, high upon a secluded hillside. Soak in the outdoor hot tub and then take advantage of the gas barbeque available to guests. Christy spoils visitors by providing a petite box of her own luscious chocolate truffles at their bedside.

Loganberry Hot Tea

Pour 3/4 ounce Whidbeys liqueur into each mug. Add 3/4 ounce Grand Marnier to each and fill with 3/4 ounce hot tea.

Bell's Strawberry Tart

2 cups flour

1/4 cup sugar

3/4 cup butter, cubed

2 egg yolks

1 (3 ounce) package
cream cheese

1 cup heavy cream

1/2 teaspoon vanilla

1/2 teaspoon lemon peel

1 teaspoon lemon juice

3 1/2 tablespoons
powdered sugar

6 cups fresh strawberries,
hulls removed

1 1/2 cups red currant
jelly

2 tablespoons kirsch

A favorite summer pastime
of Whidbey Island residents is
gathering local berries for jams,
jellies, desserts and breakfast
dishes. Strawberries, raspberries,
blackberries and loganberries
are bountiful on the island. The
owners of *Bell's Strawberry Farm*
believe they "have Whidbey
Island's finest strawberries."

Preheat oven to 300°.

In a medium bowl stir together flour and sugar. Mix in butter
with fingers until smooth. Stir in egg yolks until dough holds
together. Press dough into a 12-inch tart pan with a removable
bottom. Bake for 30 to 40 minutes until crust is golden brown.

Beat cream cheese in a bowl with an electric mixer. Gradually
blend in the cream. Add vanilla, lemon peel and lemon juice.
Beat until the mixture is like stiffly whipped cream. Add sugar
and beat until well blended. Cover and chill for up to 24 hours.

To assemble, wash the strawberries and let them dry. Boil jelly
and kirsch in a small saucepan until the jelly "sheets" from a
spoon into drops. Paint the inside of the shell with a thin coating
of glaze and allow it to set for 5 minutes. Save the rest of the
glaze. Spread the pastry cream in the bottom of the cooked pastry
shell. Place berries on cream with the largest ones in the center.
Be sure to cover the entire surface of the cream. With a spoon or
pastry brush, apply the remaining glaze over the berries, after first
warming up the glaze. Refrigerate until ready to serve, but not
longer than 3 hours.

Remove from the pan and cut into wedges to serve.

8 servings

Strawberry Delight

1 1/2 pounds strawberries
3/4 cup sugar
1/4 cup kirsch
1/4 cup heavy cream
2 large peaches

Put strawberries through blender to make 2 cups purée. Add sugar, kirsch and cream. Mix lightly. Chill in refrigerator.

Skin peaches and cut into slices. Place peach slices in individual serving dishes and spoon strawberry purée over.

6 servings

Ruby Thomas serves strawberry purée in champagne glasses crowned with fresh peach slices.

White Cloud Pie

4 egg whites
1/4 teaspoon cream of tartar
1 cup sugar
1 cup heavy cream
1/2 teaspoon vanilla
1 ounce unsweetened chocolate

Preheat oven to 275°.

Beat egg whites and cream of tartar until thick. Gradually add sugar while continuing to beat until stiff peaks form.

Spread in greased and floured pie plate. Bake for 20 minutes. Increase heat to 325° and continue cooking for 40 minutes. Cool.

Whip cream until stiff. Add vanilla and mix well. Cover meringue with cream. Top with grated chocolate.

Cover with plastic wrap and chill for 10 to 24 hours.

6 servings

A heavenly pie sent to us by Wilma Patrick.

Chocolate Raspberry Meringue Bars

1 cup softened butter

1 1/2 cups sugar

4 eggs separated, reserving 2 yolks in a small dish

2 1/2 cups flour

1 (10 ounce) jar raspberry jam

1 cup chocolate chips

2 cups finely chopped walnuts

Preheat oven to 350°.

In a large mixing bowl or food processor mix together butter, 1/2 cup sugar, and egg yolks. Add 2 1/2 cups flour; blend thoroughly. Pat the dough into a jellyroll pan or a deep cookie sheet. Bake at 350° for 20 minutes or until dough is lightly browned.

Remove pan from oven. Immediately spread jam over the warm crust. Sprinkle chocolate chips over the jam. Set aside.

In a deep mixing bowl beat 4 egg whites together until stiff. Fold in chopped nuts and 1 cup sugar. Gently spread the meringue over chocolate.

Bake bars at 350° for 25 minutes or until lightly browned. Remove from oven and allow to cool before cutting into bars.

3 dozen bars

The incredible flavors of chocolate and raspberry team together to give these bars a "mouth watering" appeal.

Europeans discovered chocolate late in the 15th century. They found it as a bitter beverage drunk by native peoples in Mexico, Central America and the Caribbean. The drink was made from cocoa seeds allowed to ferment, dried, roasted and crushed into a paste. The paste was then mixed with water and flavored with spices. Sugar, cinnamon, almonds, hazelnuts and orange were often added.

Chocolate Espresso Cake

1/4 cup very strong espresso
4 ounces semi-sweet
   chocolate chips
1/2 cup butter
1 3/4 cups brown sugar
3 eggs room temperature

1 tablespoon vanilla
3/4 cup buttermilk
1 1/2 cups flour
1/2 teaspoon baking soda
1/2 teaspoon baking powder

Raspberry Sauce

Crown this fabulous, rich chocolate cake with a layer of raspberry sauce and a nest of fresh berries.

Preheat oven to 350°.

Grease and flour a springform cake pan. Set aside.

Make espresso; set aside.

Melt chocolate in a double boiler until smooth; set aside to cool.

In a large mixing bowl, cream the butter. Add brown sugar; beat until light and fluffy (about 8 minutes). Add eggs 1 at a time. Mix in vanilla. Set aside.

In a small bowl mix cooled espresso into buttermilk. Sift the flour, baking soda and powder together. Starting with the buttermilk, alternately add buttermilk and flour mixtures to the batter. Mix well after each addition. Add the cooled chocolate to the cake batter and blend well.

Pour cake batter into the prepared pan. Bake at 350° for 1 hour. Top cooled cake with raspberry sauce and garnish individual servings with several whole raspberries.

Raspberry Sauce

1 (10 ounce) package
   frozen raspberries

1 teaspoon cornstarch
1/2 teaspoon sugar

Drain berries, reserving juice. Set berries aside. In a small saucepan stir cornstarch into juice. Heat and boil juice 1 minute. Remove from heat and cool. Gently stir raspberries into sauce mixture.

Serve raspberry sauce over chocolate espresso cake.

10 servings

Chocolate Lover's Cake

Cake

1 cup cocoa
1 cup butter, softened
2 1/2 cups sugar
4 eggs
1 1/2 teaspoons vanilla
2 3/4 cups flour
2 teaspoons baking soda
1/2 teaspoon salt
1/2 teaspoon baking powder

Liz Kline created this cake for the person who appreciates a true, deep chocolate taste. Liz has found that orange and mint are flavors that enhance the taste of chocolate. In this recipe you may choose between the Creme de Menthe filling and the Citrus Orange filling.

Preheat oven to 350°. Grease and flour 3 round 9-inch cake pans.

In a medium size bowl, combine cocoa with 2 cups of boiling water. Whisk until smooth. Cool completely.

In a large mixing bowl beat the butter, sugar, eggs and vanilla together until light (about 5 minutes).

In a separate bowl, sift the flour with the soda, salt and baking powder. With the mixer running at low speed add the flour mixture to the butter mixture, alternately, with the cocoa. Begin and end with the flour mixture. Do not overbeat. Pour the cake mix into the 3 pans.

Bake cake layers for 25-30 minutes in a 350° oven. The cake surface should spring back when gently pressed with a fingertip in the center. Cool the cake in the pans for 10 minutes. Remove from pans and cool completely on wire racks.

Creme de Menthe Filling

6 tablespoons butter, softened
3 1/2 cups powdered sugar
6 tablespoons Creme de Menthe liqueur

Beat all ingredients together in a small mixing bowl. Divide the filling evenly between the layers and top.

continued on next page

Citrus Orange Filling

6 tablespoons butter, softened

2 tablespoons grated fresh orange rind

2 1/2 cups powdered sugar

4 tablespoons orange juice

Beat all ingredients together in a small mixing bowl. Divide the filling evenly between the layers and top of cake.

Chocolate Frosting

1/2 cup butter, softened   3 cups powdered sugar

1/2 cup cocoa   1/2 cup hot coffee

In a small mixing bowl beat all ingredients together until smooth. This recipe may be cut in half for those who desire a little less frosting on the cake.

12 servings

Chocolate Mousse

1 1/2 cups half and half

1 1/2 cups semi-sweet chocolate chips

2 eggs

2 tablespoons orange liqueur

1/2 cup heavy cream, whipped

2 ounces grated milk chocolate for garnish

In a small saucepan scald the half and half over medium high heat until bubbles appear at the edge. In an electric blender mix together chocolate chips, eggs and liqueur until slightly blended. Add scalded half and half to the mixture in blender. Whip until smooth.

Pour into individual serving dishes or stemware and chill until firm. Dollop each serving with 1 tablespoon whipped cream and sprinkle with grated chocolate.

6 servings

Marge Ronhaar discovered this fabulous recipe for a velvety smooth chocolate mousse. As an alternative to the orange liqueur we also use the local loganberry flavored Whidbeys liqueur.

Red Grapes in Sherried Cream

1/3 cup sugar
2 tablespoons cornstarch
1/8 teaspoon salt
2 cups milk
1/4 cup cream sherry

2 egg yolks, slightly
  beaten
2 tablespoons butter
1 teaspoon vanilla
1 bunch red grapes

In a large saucepan stir together the sugar, cornstarch and salt. Gradually add the milk and sherry and blend well. Cook over medium heat, stirring constantly, until it boils. Boil 1 minute and remove from heat.

Stir half of the hot sauce into a bowl with the beaten egg yolks. Then, return all to the saucepan and cook for 30 more seconds. Remove from heat and stir in butter and vanilla until butter melts.

Layer spoonfuls of grapes and pudding in 4 stemmed glasses. Chill until serving time.

4 servings

Enjoy the sweet flavor and the extra crisp texture of the Red Flame seedless grape in this creamy pudding.

Victorian Amaretto Cheese Dip

2 (8 ounce) packages cream cheese
4 egg yolks
1/2 cup sugar
1/4 cup Amaretto liqueur

Combine all ingredients and cream together until smooth. Serve the dip in the middle of a platter of mixed fruit.

Yield: 1 1/2 cups

Delores Fresh, owner of the *Victorian Bed and Breakfast* in Coupeville, serves this dip with seasonal fresh fruit as a sweet alternative to a heavy dessert. Guests at the Victorian may choose from two tastefully furnished bedrooms with private baths, or hide away in the Victorian's private cottage.

Lime Cream

1 cup sugar

2 tablespoons cornstarch

1/2 teaspoon mace

1/8 teaspoon salt

1/4 cup lime juice

1 egg

1 teaspoon grated lime zest

1 teaspoon vanilla

drop of green food coloring

1 cup heavy cream, whipped

Garnish: twists or knots of lime peel and
shaved chocolate curls

Stir together sugar, cornstarch, mace and salt; add 1 cup water and cook until thickened. Add lime juice and cook 1 minute longer. Combine egg with 2 tablespoons of hot mixture, stir and add to remaining hot mixture. Cook for 1 to 2 minutes longer. Remove from heat, add lime zest, vanilla and coloring and cool.

Fold in whipped cream and serve in long stemmed glasses with twists or knots of lime peel and shaved chocolate curls for garnish.

4 servings

At the *Cliff House* in Freeland you'll enjoy a pleasant blend of stone, oriental carpets, primitive and contemporary art. Gracefully combined with sophisticated architecture you'll discover a unique setting. There is no place quite like the *Cliff House*. Lime Cream is a *Cliff House* favorite prepared by Peggy Moore and Walter O'Toole. It is especially light and luscious following a seafood or poultry entrée.

Whidbeys Decadence

Pour 1 ounce Whidbeys liqueur into each mug. Add 4 ounces hot chocolate to each. Top with whipped cream and chocolate sprinkles.

The "Very Best" Cheesecake

Cheesecake Crust

1 cup plus 2 tablespoons graham cracker crumbs
1/4 cup sugar
1/4 cup melted butter or margarine

In a bowl mix together 1 cup cracker crumbs, sugar and butter until crumbly. Lightly grease a 9-inch springform pan. Sprinkle 2 tablespoons crumbs over bottom of pan. Firmly pack cracker mixture into bottom of pan.

Cheesecake Filling

2 (8 ounce) packages cream cheese, softened at room temperature
1 teaspoon vanilla extract
1/2 cup sugar
3 eggs

Preheat oven to 375°.

Using a mixer or food processor beat cream cheese until smooth. Add vanilla, sugar and eggs; beat 10 minutes or until creamy.

Carefully pour filling over crumb crust in pan. Bake at 375° for 20 minutes. Remove from oven and cool for 15 minutes. Increase oven temperature to 475°.

Cheesecake Topping

1 pint sour cream
1/4 cup sugar
1 teaspoon vanilla extract

Stir or mix together the sour cream, sugar and vanilla until the sugar has dissolved. Spread topping evenly over the cheesecake. Bake cheesecake at 475° for 10 minutes. Remove from oven and cool at room temperature before placing in the refrigerator.

Serve cheesecake wedges topped with sliced strawberries or a dab of cherry pie filling.

8 servings

continued on next page

Your search for the perfect cheesecake may be over when you try Marie Jenkins' sublime dessert. Jane O'Kelley has tailored her aunt's cheesecake recipe to work in creating bite size cheesecakes using miniature muffin tins. These mini cheesecakes are part of a Christmas tradition in Jane's home.

The "Very Best" Cheesecake continued

Miniature Cheesecakes

Increase graham cracker crust ingredients as follows:

2 cups cracker crumbs
1/2 cup melted butter
3 tablespoons sugar

Mix all ingredients together. Press crust into greased miniature muffin tins. Bake at 375° for 5 minutes. Then, fill the crust cups with the cheesecake filling. Bake them in a 350° oven for 12 minutes. Allow cheesecakes to cool before removing from the tin. These will freeze beautifully.

Boudoir Cheesecake

3 (3 ounce) packages cream cheese
1 cup sugar
1/8 teaspoon salt
1 teaspoon lemon juice
2 eggs, separated
1 cup heavy cream, whipped
1 teaspoon vanilla
1 9-inch baked graham cracker crust
grated nutmeg for garnish

Joyce DeJong captivates guests with this cool, sensuous dessert. Freshly grated nutmeg on the top of the creamy cheesecake is a perfect and unusual garnish.

Beat together cream cheese, sugar, salt and lemon juice. Beat egg yolks; add to cheese mixture. Beat egg whites until stiff and fold into cheese mixture. Fold in whipped cream and vanilla.

Pour into pie crust and sprinkle with grated nutmeg if desired. Cover with plastic wrap and freeze.

8 servings

Washington Apple Cake

5-6 Macintosh apples

3 eggs

2 cups sugar

1 cup oil

2 cups flour

2 teaspoons cinnamon

1 teaspoon baking soda

1/2 teaspoon salt

1 teaspoon vanilla

1 cup walnuts, coarsely chopped

Cream Cheese Icing

Preheat oven to 350°.

Peel and slice apples to equal 4 cups. Layer them in the bottom of a 9 x 13-inch pan.

In a bowl beat the eggs until thick. Add the sugar and oil and beat until creamy. Mix together the dry ingredients and add them to the egg mixture. Blend in the vanilla and beat thoroughly. Stir in the nuts.

Pour the batter over the apples. Bake at 350° for 1 hour. Cool.

Cream Cheese Icing

2 (3 ounce) packages cream cheese

4 tablespoons melted butter

2 cups powdered sugar

2 teaspoons vanilla

1/4 teaspoon lemon juice

Cream all ingredients together until icing is smooth. Spread over the cake after it has cooled completely.

10 -12 servings

Everyone will rave about this wonderful apple cake! Be sure to refrigerate the cake so it will retain its fresh moistness.

Fort Ebey overlooks the Strait of Juan de Fuca on North Whidbey. The fort was once an active military structure built as part of our defense network after the attack on Pearl Harbor. It is now a beautiful state park which is popular for its hiking trails, picnic spots, surfing area, campsites and fishing. Lake Pondilla is a lovely, short walk from the fort and popular among anglers for bass fishing. The park area is also home to an abundance of wildlife, including bald eagles.

Fresh Fruit and Cream Cake

1 cup milk

2 tablespoons butter

4 eggs

2 cups sugar

1/2 teaspoon salt

2 teaspoons vanilla

2 cups flour

2 teaspoons baking powder

fresh fruit such as peaches or strawberries

1 pint heavy cream, whipped

Preheat oven to 350°.

In a small saucepan bring milk to a boil over medium heat. Add butter, then stir until it melts. Set aside.

In a large mixing bowl, beat eggs until light and fluffy. Add sugar, salt and vanilla; then stir well. Slowly add the butter and milk mixture. Quickly beat flour and baking powder into cake batter. Combine thoroughly.

Grease and flour two 9-inch round cake pans. Pour the cake batter into the pans. Bake at 350° for 25 minutes or until the cake tests firm in the center. Allow to cool.

Slice each layer in half, creating 4 thin layers. Place 1 layer on a serving plate. Cover cake with sliced fruit. Cover fruit with whipped cream. Repeat sequence of layering. Frost the top and sides of cake with whipped cream. Chill cake until serving.

10 servings

The Navy population of Oak Harbor shares an array of recipes from all over the world. Linda Jackson has many opportunities to use this North Carolina recipe for a delightful sponge cake topped with fresh fruit.

Linda often makes the cake several days before serving. It will freeze well if completely covered after the cake has cooled. Allow the cake to thaw at room temperature before layering it with fruit and whipped cream. It can be made the morning of a dinner party and refrigerated. When using peaches, squeeze lemon juice over fruit to prevent browning. Garnish the top of the cake with several slices of fruit or garnish each individual serving.

Banana Cake with Whipped Cream Frosting

2 1/4 cups flour
1 2/3 cups sugar
1 1/4 teaspoons soda
1 1/4 teaspoons baking powder
1 teaspoon salt
2/3 cup shortening

2/3 cup buttermilk
3 eggs
1 1/4 cups mashed ripe banana
2/3 cup finely chopped nuts

Whipped Cream Frosting

Preheat oven to 350°.

Grease and lightly flour 3 round 8-inch cake pans.

In a large mixing bowl, combine all ingredients together. Blend for 1 minute on low speed. Scrape the bowl occasionally and continue to beat the cake mix for 3 more minutes at high speed. Pour the mix into the 3 pans.

Bake the cake layers in a 350° oven for 35 minutes, or until it tests done in the center. Cool.

Frost between the layers, and on the top and sides of the cake, with the Whipped Cream Frosting.

Like banana bread, this cake is especially moist and rather sweet. The stovetop frosting has the consistency of whipped cream and is an agreeable complement to the banana cake.

Whipped Cream Frosting

5 tablespoons flour
1 cup milk
1/2 cup margarine
1/2 cup shortening

1 cup sugar
1/4 teaspoon salt
2 teaspoons vanilla

In a saucepan over medium heat cook the flour and milk together until thick. Cool to lukewarm.

In a separate bowl, beat together the margarine, shortening, sugar, salt and vanilla.

Add the flour and milk mixture and beat until the mixture has the consistency of whipped cream.

12 servings

Italian Cream Cake

1/2 cup shortening

1 cup margarine

2 cups sugar

1 teaspoon vanilla

5 eggs, separated

1 teaspoon soda

2 cups flour

1 cup buttermilk

2 cups coconut

1 cup chopped pecans

Cream Cheese Filling

Preheat oven to 350°.

Mix shortening, margarine, sugar and vanilla. Add egg yolks, one at a time. Mix in soda and flour alternately with the buttermilk. Stir in coconut and pecans.

Beat egg whites until stiff. Fold egg whites into batter. Bake in 3 greased and floured 8-inch round cake pans at 350° for 30 minutes.

Spread filling between cooled layers and over top of cake.

Cream Cheese Filling

1 cup margarine

1 (8 ounce) package cream cheese

1 pound powdered sugar

1 teaspoon vanilla

1 cup chopped pecans

Blend margarine with cream cheese; add sugar and vanilla. Mix in pecans.

12 servings

Ray Zylstra will occasionally surprise his friends with this lightly flavored coconut cake.

Cappuccino Whidbeys

Pour 1 ounce Whidbeys liqueur into each mug. Add coffee to the Whidbeys. Top with whipped cream and shaved chocolate.

Jan Hagel, Olie Bollen and Dutch Coffee

Jan Hagel

1 egg, separated
1/2 pound butter, softened
1 cup sugar

1/2 teaspoon cinnamon
2 cups flour
1/3 cup chopped walnuts

Preheat oven to 375°.

In a mixing bowl combine the egg yolk with the butter, sugar, cinnamon and flour. Mix thoroughly. Add walnuts. Spread dough in a greased 8-inch square pan. In a separate dish froth the egg white with a wire wisk and spread on top of the dough.

Bake Jan Hagel at 375° for 15-20 minutes. Cut into bars while slightly warm.

12 bars

Dutch Coffee

Place a cinnamon stick in each coffee mug. Fill with freshly brewed black coffee, stir in 1 tablespoon heavy cream, and float a pat of butter on top. Serve with sugar.

Olie Bollen

2 tablespoons plus 1 cup sugar
2 packages yeast
2 cups raisins
2 cups currants
5 eggs

2 cups scalded milk
1/2 cup margarine, softened
10 cups flour
1 cup sugar
1 1/2 teaspoons salt

Dissolve 2 tablespoons sugar in 1 cup warm water. Sprinkle yeast into water. Let this stand while preparing dough.

In a small bowl cover raisins and currants with hot water. Set aside.

continued on next page

Jan Hagel and Olie Bollen are delicious components of warm, Dutch hospitality. Savor an afternoon break with friends when you serve Dutch pastries and a cup of sweetened "Dutch" coffee.

Olie Bollen continued

In a large mixing bowl beat eggs slightly. Add milk, 1 1/2 cups water, yeast mixture and margarine. Add flour, sugar and salt. Drain raisins and currants; add to dough mixture. Beat well.

Let the dough rise in a warm place until it doubles in size. Punch the dough back into the bowl and allow to rise once again.

Fill a fryer pot with oil that is 4 inches deep. Melted Crisco works very well for frying the Olie Bollen. Scoop out large spoonfuls of dough and drop into the hot oil. Turn them gently for even frying until each one is golden brown. Prick them to ensure they are fully cooked inside. If the oil is too hot the Olie Bollen will only cook quickly on the outside and not in the inside. Drain on a paper towel and roll each one in a bowl of granulated sugar.

24 rolls

Snow Caps

4 squares unsweetened
   chocolate

1/2 cup butter

2 cups sugar

4 eggs

2 cups flour

2 teaspoons baking
   powder

1/4 teaspoon salt

1 teaspoon vanilla

2 cups powdered sugar

This recipe produces a cookie that is popular in the Moore and Skinner households.

Preheat oven to 350°.

Melt chocolate with butter. Cool and mix in sugar. In a large bowl, beat the eggs. In a separate bowl, combine flour, baking powder and salt. Alternately stir chocolate and flour mixtures into beaten eggs. Add vanilla and chill for several hours.

Form dough into walnut sized balls. Roll in powdered sugar. Bake on greased sheets at 350° for 10-12 minutes.

3 dozen cookies

Almond Bars

1 box yellow cake mix

3 eggs

1/2 cup plus 1 teaspoon butter

1 cup chopped pecans or walnuts

1 (8 ounce) package softened cream cheese

1 (1 pound) box powdered sugar

1 teaspoon almond extract

1 teaspoon vanilla

Preheat oven to 325°.

In a large mixing bowl or food processor blend the cake mix, 1 egg and 1/2 cup butter together. Pat mixture into a 9 x 13-inch pan. Sprinkle top of crust with chopped nuts.

In a large mixing bowl or food processor blend 2 eggs, cream cheese, powdered sugar, 1 teaspoon butter and both extracts. Pour this mixture over the crust in the pan.

Bake the Almond Bars at 325° for 40 minutes. Allow to cool in the pan overnight, or for several hours.

20 bars

These delicious bars are best when made a day in advance which allows them to set properly. Susan Waller has taken these Almond Bars to countless functions and they are always a hit.

The ancient Greeks considered almonds to be a symbol of fertility and the Moslems considered them the mark of heavenly hope.

Bears Chocolate Chip Cookies

1 cup cold unsalted butter, cut into chunks

1 cup firmly packed brown sugar

3/4 cup sugar

1 teaspoon salt (optional)

2 eggs

1 1/2 teaspoons vanilla

2 1/2 cups flour

1 1/4 teaspoons baking soda

3 cups chocolate chips

2 cups chopped walnuts

In a large bowl, beat butter, sugars and salt until no butter flecks remain. Beat in eggs and vanilla until well blended. Add flour and soda and blend well. Stir in chocolate chips and walnuts.

Shape dough into 1 1/2 inch balls, using about 2 1/2 tablespoons dough for each. Place each ball evenly spaced on an ungreased baking sheet. Cover and chill for at least 6 hours or up to 3 days.

Flatten each ball into a 3/4 inch thick round with straight sides. Depress center of each round slightly and let warm to room temperature.

Preheat oven to 400°.

Bake for 8 to 10 minutes or until golden brown on the edges and center is pale.

3 dozen cookies

Sid Parker shares an American favorite . . .

The word chocolate comes from the Aztec word xocoatl, meaning bitter water.

Oatmeal Raisin Cookies

3 eggs, well beaten
1 cup raisins
1 teaspoon vanilla
1 cup butter
1 cup brown sugar
1 cup white sugar
1 teaspoon salt
1 teaspoon cinnamon
2 teaspoons baking soda
2 1/2 cups flour
2 cups oatmeal
3/4 cup chopped pecans

Preheat oven to 350°.

In a small bowl, combine the eggs, raisins and vanilla making sure the raisins are well covered with the eggs. Cover the bowl with plastic wrap and allow to soak for 1 hour.

In a large mixing bowl cream the butter with the sugars. Add salt, cinnamon, soda and flour. Mix thoroughly.

Blend the egg and raisin mixture and the oatmeal into the cookie dough. Add the nuts and stir.

Drop the cookies onto a greased cookie sheet by large spoonfuls. Bake cookies at 350° for 10-12 minutes. Cool on a wire rack and serve.

2 dozen

You'll catch their hands in the cookie jar when it's filled with these chewy oatmeal cookies. This recipe is from the kitchen of Kim Skinner.

Will Jenne House
Coupeville

Whidbey Island Race Week Breakfast

Each July *Yachting Magazine* sponsors a sailing race week in the Whidbey waters. This is one of 20 races like it in the United States. About 120 boats sail out of the Oak Harbor Marina to compete in the event. Sailing enthusiasts come from several countries to participate in the activities on and off the water. There are nightly awards parties, music and other festivities at the end of each day.

Country Cottage Parfait

Scrambled Eggs with Smoked Salmon

Butterhorns

Refrigerator Bran Muffins

Carrot Pineapple Bread

NAS Whidbey Intruder/Prowler Brunch ("After the ball")

Whidbey Island is home to Whidbey Island Naval Air Station located on North Whidbey. The mission of the air station is support for naval aviation forces. It is home to two important carrier based aircraft: the A-6E Intruder attack bomber and the tactical jamming EA-6B Prowler. The station is also the center of activity for Naval and Marine Air Reserve training activities in the Northwest. In addition, Navy Search and Rescue aids civil authorities when requested.

Orange Frappé

Potato Torte

Asparagus with Raspberry Mousseline

Oatmeal Squash Bread

Chocolate Dipped Strawberries

Frozen Lemon Delight

Coconut Date Muffins

2 large eggs
1/4 cup vegetable oil
1 cup milk
1/2 cup brown sugar
1/2 teaspoon salt
1 teaspoon nutmeg
1 teaspoon coriander
4 teaspoons baking powder
2 cups flour
3/4 cup oat bran
1/2 cup chopped dates
3/4 cup coconut
1/2 cup chopped walnuts

Preheat oven to 375°.

In a large mixing bowl beat together the eggs, oil, milk and brown sugar. Stir in the dry ingredients and mix well. Add the dates, coconut and walnuts to the batter and stir through.

Fill 12 muffin cups. Bake at 375° for 20 minutes or until they test done and are lightly browned.

12 muffins

Indulge yourself in the country charm of the *Colonel Crockett Farm Bed and Breakfast Inn* overlooking Admiralty Bay. Built around 1855, the Inn is on the National Register of Historic places and offers 5 bedrooms named after Whidbey pioneer families who held original land grants. Hosts Bob and Beulah Whitlow have filled the home with stately antiques, treasured mementos and pictures of the original homeowner's descendents. Stroll through the surrounding acres of lawn, orchard and lovely flower beds as you admire the scenery and imagine days gone by.

Coriander is an interesting herb that is normally used when fresh since it does not dry well. However, it freezes nicely, and will provide full flavor when added to your cooking at the very last stage. Coriander is known as "Chinese parsley" and is used a great deal in China and India.

Refrigerator Bran Muffins

3 cups Kelloggs All Bran
2 eggs, slightly beaten
2 cups buttermilk
1/2 cup salad oil
1 cup raisins
2 1/2 teaspoons baking soda
1 cup sugar
2 1/2 cups flour
1/2 teaspoon salt (optional)

Preheat oven to 400°.

Mix bran with 1 cup boiling water; cool completely. When the bran has cooled, add eggs, buttermilk, oil and raisins. Stir until well blended. In a separate bowl mix soda, sugar, flour and salt. Then, stir this dry mix into the bran mixture. Blend well.

To bake, spoon the batter into a well greased muffin tin. Bake at 400° for 20 minutes.

The bran batter may be stored in a tightly covered container in the refrigerator for 2-3 weeks.

2 dozen muffins

Dean and Lori Adams, the owners of *The Lovely Cottage* in Clinton, invite you to discover one of the earliest homesteads on Whidbey Island. The secluded cottage is located on the water with spectacular views of Puget Sound and the Olympic Mountains. The spacious yard features a stairway to a private beach and a luxurious outdoor hot tub.

Your hostess, Wilma O'Nan, prepares fresh fruit garnished with mint and berries from their abundant garden, served with moist Refrigerator Bran Muffins.

"Enjoy hospitality Whidbey-style, then return home; a shell in your pocket, an Island in your heart."

Whidbey Island Bed and Breakfast Association

Oatmeal Squash Bread

1 cup flour

2 teaspoons baking powder

1 teaspoon salt

1/4 teaspoon soda

1/2 teaspoon cinnamon

1/4 teaspoon ginger

1/4 teaspoon cloves

1 cup brown sugar

1 cup quick or old-fashioned oats, uncooked

1/3 cup nuts

1 egg, beaten

1/4 cup vegetable oil

1/3 cup milk

1 cup cooked Hubbard squash

Preheat oven to 350°.

Mix together all dry ingredients including sugar, oats and nuts. Add egg, oil and milk and stir until dry ingredients are moistened. Blend in squash.

Pour into a greased loaf pan. Bake at 350° for 55 to 60 minutes. Cool on a wire rack 10 minutes before removing from pan. Cool, wrap and store one day before serving.

1 loaf

This bread is surprisingly rich and moist and is wonderful when served late in the morning or for afternoon tea. To attain the full bodied flavor, Jean Sherman wraps the cooled bread and lays it aside a day before slicing and serving.

In the mid 1800s early settlers on Whidbey Island built blockhouses as protection against Indian attack. Four of these blockhouses still stand, one in downtown Coupeville and the others nearby.

Carrot Pineapple Bread

1 1/4 cups vegetable oil

2 cups sugar

2 eggs

3 cups flour

1 teaspoon soda

3 teaspoons cinnamon

1 teaspoon salt

2 teaspoons vanilla

1 (8 ounce) can crushed pineapple

2 cups grated carrots

1 cup chopped nuts

Preheat oven to 350°.

Cream the oil and sugar together in a large mixing bowl. Add the eggs and mix until smooth. Add dry ingredients and vanilla alternately with pineapple to the bread batter. Fold in grated carrots and nuts.

Pour into a greased loaf pan and bake in a 350° oven for 1 hour. Cool slightly before removing bread from pan.

Finish cooling on wire rack before slicing.

1 loaf

This unusual combination of fruits and vegetable create a moist bread with a character all its own. It bakes to a rich brown and is delicious when served warm or cold.

To keep breads warm, heat an unglazed ceramic tile by immersing it in very hot water for a few minutes. Dry it off and wrap it in a cloth napkin. Place the tile in the bottom of a basket and it will keep your baked bread toasty warm.

Beach House Lemon Tea Bread

1/3 cup butter

1 cup sugar

3 tablespoons lemon extract

2 eggs

1 1/2 cups flour

1 teaspoon baking powder

1/2 teaspoon salt

1/2 cup milk

1 1/2 tablespoons grated lemon rind

1/2 cup chopped pecans or walnuts, optional

Preheat oven to 350°.

In a food processor or mixer, blend together the butter, sugar and lemon extract. Add eggs and process until smooth.

Sift the flour, baking powder and salt together; add to the butter mixture, alternately, with the milk. Mix lightly between additions and blend until smooth. Add grated rind to the bread mixture, and add nuts if desired.

Pour the batter into a greased loaf pan. Bake at 350° for 45 minutes or until a toothpick inserted in the middle of the bread comes out clean. Allow the bread to cool for 10 minutes before removing from pan. Cool on a wire rack if possible.

Wrap the bread tightly in foil to store. When the bread is wrapped well it will remain fresh in the freezer for up to 6 weeks.

1 loaf

Guests at Judy Thorsen's *Beach House Bed and Breakfast Inn* enjoy a continental breakfast each morning as they watch the ships traverse Useless Bay. Many visitors spend their afternoons swimming or sunning on the sandy beach, or digging clams on the nearby tideflats.

Discover a unique part of South Whidbey when you visit Useless Bay. This bay is a wetland providing a natural habitat for aquatic and land animal species. It is also a place of abundant plant life in the marshland. There are several environmental groups that carefully monitor Useless Bay in order to protect the delicate balance between all plant and animal life.

Banana Bread

1/4 cup margarine

1 cup firmly packed dark brown sugar

1 egg

1 1/2 cups flour

1 teaspoon salt

1 teaspoon baking soda

1 cup mashed, ripe banana (approximately 2 large bananas)

Preheat oven to 325°.

Melt the margarine and set aside to cool. Beat the egg and sugar together. Add cooled margarine. Stir the flour, salt and soda together. Alternately add the dry ingredients and mashed banana to butter mixture. Mix until moist. Pour the batter into a greased and floured loaf pan.

Bake at 325° for 60 minutes or until a pick inserted in the center of the bread comes out clean.

Allow the bread to cool for several minutes before removing from the pan.

1 loaf

The secret to this delicious and unique Banana Bread is the use of dark brown sugar.

To add variety to Banana Bread, add 1 cup finely chopped dried apricots; 1 cup cranberries; 1 cup finely chopped, pitted dried prunes; or 1 cup dark seedless raisins.

Dilly Bread

1 1/2 cups small curd cottage cheese

1/2 cup sugar

1/2 cup oil

1 teaspoon salt

2 packages yeast

2 cups milk

1 cup wheat germ

1/2 cup corn meal

1 cup milled bran

1/2 cup whole wheat or graham flour

1/4 cup dry onion or 1 cup chopped fresh onion
(optional)

3 cups white flour

2 tablespoons dill weed

In a small saucepan, heat the cottage cheese slowly over low heat. Add sugar, oil and salt to cottage cheese. Set aside.

Dissolve yeast in 1/2 cup warm water. Heat the milk over low heat; add milk to the yeast. Stir the dry ingredients, including onion, into the yeast mixture. Add cottage cheese mixture and blend thoroughly.

Knead the dough until elastic. Allow the dough to rise in a warm place until it doubles in size. Divide the dough into 2 balls and place each in a greased loaf pan. Let the dough rise a second time until it doubles in size.

Preheat oven to 350°.

Bake Dilly Bread at 350° for 35 minutes or until the loaves sound hollow when tapped.

For fullest flavor, serve Dilly Bread while warm.

2 loaves

Baking bread "from scratch" is a gratifying experience for any cook. Debbie's grandmother, Reka Poole, often brings warm Dilly Bread to family gatherings.

Bread should be stored at room temperature. Although bread stored in the refrigerator will be less likely to have mold growth, it will become stale more quickly.

Dutch Roggebrood Bread (Rye Bread)

2 cups cracked wheat cereal

3/4 cup dark molasses

1 teaspoon soda

1 teaspoon salt

1 1/2 cups white flour

Preheat oven to 325°.

In a small bowl soak the wheat cereal in 2 cups hot water for 1 hour.

In a larger mixing bowl add the cereal mixture to the molasses, soda and salt. Add flour and blend well.

Pour the bread dough into a greased loaf pan and cover with foil. Bake at 325° for 1 1/2 hours.

1 loaf

This recipe has always been a favorite passed among Oak Harbor's Dutch community. The rye bread is dense, but excellent when served with slices of Gouda cheese or sharp cheddar.

Beer Bread

3 cups self-rising flour

2 tablespoons sugar

1 (12 ounce) bottle of beer, at room temperature

1/4 cup margarine, melted

Preheat oven to 375°.

Stir together flour, sugar and beer. Pour into a greased loaf pan and pour melted margarine over top.

Bake at 375° for 65 minutes.

1 loaf

Beer Bread is a beautifully browned bread with a robust flavor. Try baking this bread in a natural terra cotta loaf pan, "old world style." The pan retains heat well and distributes it evenly. This feature provides bread with a golden crisp bottom and side crusts and a moist inner texture.

Four Seed Crunchy Bread

2 packages active dry yeast

1/4 cup molasses or honey

1/4 cup oil

1/2 teaspoon salt

4 1/2 cups whole wheat flour

1/2 cup sunflower seeds

1/2 cup millet

1/4 cup sesame seeds

2 tablespoons poppy seeds

Combine yeast, molasses or honey and 1 3/4 cups water in a bowl for 5 minutes. Add oil, salt and 3 cups flour. Beat with an electric mixer on medium for 5 minutes. Mix in all seeds.

Turn dough out onto a board coated with 1 1/2 cups flour. Knead until smooth and satiny, adding more flour if needed. Shape dough into a loaf and place in greased loaf pan. Cover and let rise until dough is about 1 inch above rim, 30 to 40 minutes.

Preheat oven to 350°.

Bake at 350° for 40 minutes or until the loaf is browned and sounds hollow when tapped.

1 loaf

On blustery autumn afternoons we like to sail to Coupeville. Our picnic often includes a warm nourishing soup and this crunchy bread.

Soft-crusted breads should be wrapped tightly in plastic wrap or placed in an airtight bag. Breads with a crisp crust, such as French, should be wrapped loosely.

Laura's Baguettes

1 package dry yeast
3 1/2 cups flour
2 teaspoons salt
1 egg, beaten with 1 teaspoon water

Sprinkle the yeast over 1/3 cup warm water; mix and set aside. When the yeast has dissolved, add flour, salt and 1 1/4 cups water. Stir to mix well.

Turn the dough onto a floured surface and knead until smooth (about 10 minutes). Place the dough in a bowl and let rise in a warm spot for 1 1/2 hours until the dough has doubled in size.

Punch the dough down and let it rise again for 15 minutes.

Shape the dough into 2 long round loaves and place in a greased baguette pan or on a greased baking sheet. Allow the loaves to rise 1 hour more.

Before preheating oven to 375°, fill a 9 x 13-inch baking pan with water. Place pan on lower shelf of oven.

Brush the egg wash on raised loaves. Bake at 375° for 30 minutes. Loaves should be golden brown and sound hollow when tapped.

2 loaves

Traditionally, French bread is eaten "au natural" with chunks pulled from the freshly baked loaf. This fragrant, warm bread can be a meal in itself.

The long bladed slicing knife intended for meats is also a good bread knife. Turn fresh loaves of crusty bread to their side and slice them from the side (as opposed to the top of the loaf). This method will make the job of slicing less difficult since it is easier to guide the knife when slicing from the side.

Yeast Rolls

1 package dry yeast
1/3 cup sugar
3 cups flour
3/4 teaspoon salt
2 tablespoons oil

Dissolve yeast in 1/3 cup warm water. Add 1 cup warm water, sugar and flour. Mix together to make a stiff dough.

Set aside and let rise 1 hour or until double in bulk.

Stir batter down and stir in salt and oil. Turn onto a floured board and knead for 3 minutes. Shape dough into 24 balls and place 2, side by side, in each greased cup of a muffin pan. Cover with a towel and allow to rise 1 hour.

Preheat oven to 325°.

Bake at 325° for 20 minutes or until golden brown. Pat warm rolls with French Herb Butter or Honey Butter found on page 182.

12 rolls

These rolls are not as time consuming as you may think. The actual working time to prepare Yeast Rolls is about 20 minutes. The mouth watering aroma will attract your family to the heart of the home . . . your kitchen.

Stale bread can be very useful for croutons. Cut the bread into pieces the size of dice. Place them in a 325° oven for 15 minutes to dry. Brush both sides of the croutons with olive oil. Sprinkle with herbs or cut garlic, if desired. Bake another 15 minutes until barely brown in color.

Butters

French Herb Butter

1 teaspoon lemon juice
1/2 cup butter, softened at room temperature
2 teaspoons chives, finely chopped
1 teaspoon crushed dried parsley flakes
1 teaspoon dried basil

Add lemon juice to softened butter. Gradually stir in dried herbs. Spoon into a small butter tub; cover and store in the refrigerator for up to 3 weeks.

This is a traditional butter from France which is delicious on bread, and fun to use on popcorn. Make the butter at least one day ahead of serving to allow the flavors a chance to mellow.

Spicy Butter

1/2 cup butter or margarine
3 tablespoons firmly packed brown sugar
1/4 teaspoon cinnamon
1/4 teaspoon allspice
1/4 teaspoon nutmeg

Whip butter or margarine until fluffy with a food processor or electric mixer.

Add sugar and spices until evenly mixed.

Place in an airtight container and store in the refrigerator.

Spicy Butter is delicious served on French toast, waffles and pancakes.

Honey Butter

1 cube butter, softened
1/3 cup honey
Dash of cinnamon and nutmeg and/or orange zest
    (optional)

Cream butter. Blend in remaining ingredients. Spoon into a small crock and refrigerate.

Fruits Gourmands

1 whole cantaloupe
1/2 cup fresh strawberries
1 whole kiwi
1 teaspoon lemon juice
4 large cooking apples
2 tablespoons brown sugar
1 teaspoon cinnamon
dash of ground cloves

Cut the cantaloupe in half through the center; discard the seeds, and set aside the 2 halves. Clean and cut the strawberries in half. Peel the kiwi and slice lengthwise, making thin slices. Refrigerate the cantaloupe, strawberries and kiwi.

Fill a shallow pan with 1 inch cold water. Add the lemon juice. Core, peel and slice apples; immediately immerse slices in the lemon water. When all apples are sliced, discard most of the water except 2 tablespoons which needs to remain in the pan with the apples. Sprinkle the brown sugar, cinnamon and cloves over the apples.

Put apple slices in a saucepan. Cook them over medium heat for 30 minutes or until the water has almost evaporated. Set aside to cool.

When ready to serve, place the cantaloupe halves in the center of 2 plates and fill them with the cooked apples. Garnish the filled cantaloupes with slices of strawberries and kiwi.

2 servings

Relax in serenity at *Pillars By The Sea* in Freeland. This farmhouse built in the early 1900s, once a roaring dance hall, is now a Bed and Breakfast Inn operated by Richard and Andrée Ploss. *Pillars By The Sea* provides a peaceful retreat on the shores of Holmes Harbor.

Chocolate Dipped Strawberries

1 pint strawberries (about 24), rinsed and dry
1 (6 ounce) package semi-sweet chocolate pieces
2 teaspoons vegetable shortening

Strawberries should be rinsed, completely dry and at room temperature for dipping. Leave hulls on.

Melt chocolate pieces in the top of a double boiler pan. Stir in the shortening until the mixture is smooth.

Hold each berry by its stem or leaves and dip one at a time, into the chocolate. Cover two thirds of the berry. A short wooden kabob stick inserted into the berry at the hull can simplify dipping. Shake the berry lightly to remove excess chocolate. Place on waxed paper or foil to set.

Spoil yourself with an elegant treat early in the morning!

Strawberries Devonshire

1 pint strawberries
1 cup sour cream
1/4 cup powdered sugar
juice from 1/2 lemon
1/2 cup brown sugar for garnish

Rinse and dry strawberries, leaving the hulls intact.

Mix the sour cream, powdered sugar and lemon juice together. Transfer to a small serving dish.

Arrange the strawberries on a platter with devonshire cream in a separate bowl. Offer the brown sugar in another small bowl as garnish. Dip the berries into the devonshire cream and then into the brown sugar.

Strawberries Devonshire is another delightful way to serve fresh strawberries.

Island Pears

1 pear
2 tablespoons cream cheese, softened
1 tablespoon honey
1/4 teaspoon vanilla
Fresh mint leaves and pansies for garnish

Split and core pear. Place skin-side-up on a microwave-proof dish. Add 1 teaspoon water to dish and cover tightly with plastic wrap. Cook in microwave on high for 2 to 3 minutes until soft.

Prepare filling by combining cream cheese, honey and vanilla.

Spoon 1 1/2 tablespoons filling into the hollow of each warm pear half and serve.

2 servings

Home By the Sea in Clinton offers the perfect opportunity to take advantage of Whidbey's quiet moments. Guests enjoy the choice of three cottages near the sandy beach; each with its own distinct personality. Sharon Fritts-Drew delights her patrons with this enchanting breakfast dish garnished with fresh mint and pansy blooms.

Hot Baked Fruit

8 ounces pitted prunes
8 ounces dried apricots
1 (13 ounce) can pineapple chunks, undrained
1 (1 pound) can cherry pie filling
1/4 cup dry sherry
1/3 cup slivered almonds

Preheat oven to 350°.

Mix prunes, apricots and pineapple in a deep casserole dish. In a separate bowl, blend the pie filling and sherry with 1 cup water; pour over the fruit. Mix thoroughly. Stir the almonds into the fruit mixture.

Cover fruit and bake at 350° for 1 1/2 hours.

Spoon baked fruit into individual sherbet dishes.

10 servings

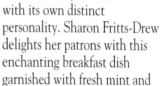

Hot Baked Fruit has become a tradition in Betty McKenzie's home during Christmas. Betty makes this dish ahead because it freezes beautifully.

Country Cottage Breakfast

5 eggs
3/4 cup milk
1/3 cup flour
1/2 teaspoon baking powder
1 (4 ounce) can diced Ortega chiles
1 cup sliced fresh mushrooms
2 1/2 cups cheddar cheese, grated
2 1/2 cups Monterey Jack cheese, grated

Preheat oven to 375°.

In a large bowl mix together the eggs, milk, flour, baking powder and chiles. Stir well.

Sauté the mushrooms until tender. Fold the mushrooms and grated cheeses into the mixture.

Pour the egg mixture into a buttered casserole or quiche dish and bake at 375° for 45 minutes. Allow to set 10 minutes before cutting and serving.

6 servings

Those who visit the *Country Cottage* in Langley will experience Trudy and Whitey Martin's true hospitality in country elegance. The following recipes are part of a full breakfast Trudy serves to guests in the sun room, dining room or under the gazebo on the deck overlooking Saratoga Passage.

Breakfast Parfait

2 cups fresh fruit, cut in small pieces
1 cup plain yogurt
2 tablespoons honey
1 1/2 cups chunky granola

In a small bowl sweeten the yogurt with the honey.

In tall crystal or parfait glasses layer the granola, fruit, and sweetened yogurt forming two layers of each ingredient in the stemware.

4 servings

Another *Country Cottage* favorite.

Eagle's Nest Zesty Eggs

1 cup milk

2 tablespoons flour

2 tablespoons margarine

1/4 teaspoon dry mustard

1/4 teaspoon onion salt

1 1/3 cups grated sharp cheddar cheese

6 eggs

Lawry's seasoned salt and pepper to taste

1/4 cup finely chopped green onion

24 Ritz crackers, crushed

Preheat oven to 350°.

In a small saucepan cook the milk, flour, margarine, mustard and salt over medium heat until a thickened white sauce is formed. Stir in 1 cup of the grated cheese until it melts. Whisk together evenly.

Place 1 heaping tablespoon cheese sauce in 6 individual ramekin dishes. Drape 1 egg over the cheese sauce in each dish. Sprinkle eggs with seasoned salt, pepper, remaining 1/3 cup grated cheese and a pinch of green onion. Sprinkle 1 1/2 tablespoons crushed Ritz crackers over each ramekin.

Bake eggs at 350° for 13-15 minutes, or until egg white is set. The eggs will continue to cook in the hot ramekin, so don't overbake.

Serve immediately.

6 servings

This recipe was provided by Nancy and Dale Bowman, owners of *Eagle's Nest Inn* in Langley. Visitors to the *Eagle's Nest Inn* are treated to the majestic view of Saratoga Passage, Camano Island and Mt. Baker. If you have the opportunity to stay at *Eagle's Nest Inn*, be sure to finish your day in their outdoor spa; then relax in the elegant guests' lounge.

"The night shall be filled with music
    And the cares that infest the day
    Shall fold their tents like the Arabs,
    And as silently steal away."

    – Henry Wadsworth Longfellow

Eggs Portugal

1 1/2 pounds sausage links

8 slices bread, crusts removed

3/4 pound cheddar cheese, grated

4 eggs

2 1/2 cups milk

1/2 teaspoon salt

3/4 tablespoon prepared mustard

1 can cream of mushroom soup

1/4 cup dry Vermouth

1 (4 ounce) can sliced mushrooms, or 1/2 cup fresh
   mushrooms, sliced and sautéed

Cut the sausage links in fourths and brown in a skillet. Drain on paper towels.

Cube the bread and place in a buttered 9 x 13-inch baking dish. Top the bread with sausage and cheese.

In a bowl, slightly beat eggs; add remaining ingredients. Blend thoroughly and pour the egg mixture over the bread mixture in the baking dish.

Cover and refrigerate overnight, or wrap tightly and freeze.

Eggs Portugal may be taken directly from the refrigerator or freezer and baked at 300° for 1 1/2 hours. Let stand 5-7 minutes before cutting in squares for serving.

10 servings

Every cook needs a recipe like this one. Use it for special occasions, or when you need a "do ahead" breakfast, brunch or luncheon. Joy Anderson prepares this egg dish the night before she cruises toward the San Juan Islands aboard her boat.

Greg and Elizabeth Osenbach have learned to appreciate the efforts and help of family and friends during harvest time at Whidbey Island Vineyard in Langley. As owners of Whidbey's first operating family vineyard, Greg and Elizabeth take great pride in their grapes and in their finished product. After trying their varieties of wine, we think you'll agree that their pride is well deserved. We suggest you try their Rhubarb wine. The wine carries a faint, but distinct aroma of rhubarb and provides a sweetly pleasant aftertaste of the fruit.

San de Fuca Eggs

4 croissants cut in half horizontally

12-18 asparagus spears, tough ends removed

3/4 pound shelled cooked crab

8 poached eggs (one per person)

Hollandaise Sauce

Preheat oven to 375°.

Set and cover the croissants on a baking sheet in a 375° oven to warm. Leave them in for about 8 minutes.

Bring 1 1/2 inch water to a boil in a large skillet. Add asparagus; cook until stems are tender, 5-7 minutes.

Place a croissant half on each individual plate. Cover croissants with crab. Put 2 or 3 asparagus spears on top of the crab. Using a slotted spoon, place 1 egg on each croissant half. Pour sauce over each croissant.

This combination of crab, asparagus, eggs and croissants is absolutely outstanding. Dollop each croissant with the subtle, yet tangy, hollandaise sauce and create a perfect entrée for late morning brunch on a Whidbey weekend.

Hollandaise Sauce

2 egg yolks

2 tablespoons lemon juice

3/4 cup melted butter

In a blender or food processor, blend the egg yolks and lemon juice. While the motor is running, slowly pour the melted butter into the yolk mixture. Serve with San de Fuca Eggs.

8 servings

The Hollandaise can be made ahead of time and stored in the refrigerator. Just before serving, place the sauce in a small metal bowl. Put the metal bowl in the center of a larger bowl to which a cup of very hot water has been added. Stir through the sauce several times while it reheats in the metal bowl (about 10 minutes).

Soufflé Pillars

1 cup Stove Top Stuffing mix
2 1/2 tablespoons flour
1 (4 ounce) can mushroom bits and pieces
1/3 cup thinly sliced sweet onion
1/3 cup thinly sliced green pepper
1 medium zucchini, peeled, sliced and cut in fourths
1/2 cup Swiss cheese, grated
6 eggs
2 1/2 cups milk

Preheat oven to 350°.

Lightly oil a 2-quart baking dish. Spread the stuffing mix in the baking dish. Sprinkle flour over stuffing. Alternately layer mushrooms, onion and pepper over the stuffing. Cover vegetables with zucchini slices. Sprinkle grated cheese over top. Set aside.

In a small bowl slightly beat the eggs. Add 1 teaspoon of the stuffing mix seasoning packet. Mix thoroughly. Add milk to the egg mixture and beat well. Pour egg mixture over the top of the vegetables in the baking dish.

Bake Soufflé Pillars for 1 hour at 350°, or until a toothpick comes out clean when inserted in the middle of the soufflé. Do not overcook.

Let the soufflé stand for 10 minutes before serving.

8 servings

Richard and Andrée Ploss invite you to experience "home away from home" as you relax in the serene environment of *Pillars By The Sea*. This Bed and Breakfast Inn is located on Holmes Harbor. Andrée serves a complete breakfast upon china plates with sterling silverware and cranberry goblets. Soufflé Pillars is one of her specialties.

"Hospitality consists of a little fire, a little food, and an immense quiet."

– Ralph Waldo Emerson
"Journals," 1856

Orange Frappé

1 (6 ounce) can frozen orange juice concentrate
1/4 cup sugar
1 cup milk
1 teaspoon vanilla
12 ice cubes

Put all ingredients in an electric blender with 1 cup water. Whip until ice is crushed. Pour into chilled glasses.

6 servings

Wake up to this luscious beverage for the beginning of a delightful day.

Smoked Salmon with Scrambled Eggs

6 eggs
1/2 cup plus 2 tablespoons milk
freshly ground pepper to taste
4 tablespoons butter
1/2 cup thin strips of smoked salmon

In a small bowl, beat the eggs with the milk and black pepper. Melt the butter in a skillet over medium heat. Pour in the egg mixture and gently scramble. Add the salmon strips just before the eggs have finished cooking.

Serve scrambled eggs immediately.

4 servings

Jim Seabolt serves this dish with toasted dark bread and radish roses.

Potato Torte

4 large baking potatoes
1/2 pound Gruyère cheese
1 pound baked ham
1 large sweet red pepper
1 egg plus 2 egg yolks
4 cups heavy cream
1 teaspoon salt
1/2 teaspoon freshly ground black pepper
1 (10 ounce) package frozen chopped spinach
1 medium onion, minced
1 tablespoon Dijon mustard

Peel potatoes; slice thin and set aside in a large bowl of cool water. Grate the Gruyère and set aside. Slice ham and red pepper into thin strips.

Combine the whole egg, yolks, cream, and salt and pepper in a large bowl. Drain the potatoes and add to the cream mixture.

Thaw and drain spinach well. In a small bowl, combine spinach with onion and mustard.

Preheat oven to 325°.

Place a thin layer of potatoes and cheese over the bottom of a buttered 9 x 13-inch casserole. Drizzle a small amount of the cream mixture over the potatoes and cheese. Top with ham strips.

Make a second layer of potatoes, cheese and cream. Top this with the spinach mixture.

Spread remaining potatoes, cheese and cream over spinach mixture. Top with strips of red pepper.

Bake the torte in a 325° oven for 2 hours. Do not cover. The top should be well browned.

Cut into squares and serve.

12 servings

This torte is a great choice for brunch since it can be made a day ahead.

Cottage Cheese Hotcakes

4 eggs, separated
3/4 cup small curd cottage cheese
1/4 cup flour
1/4 teaspoon salt
sour cream and jam

In a small bowl, beat the egg yolks until thick. Add the cottage cheese and beat well. Stir in the flour and salt. In a separate bowl, beat the egg whites until stiff and fold into the cottage cheese mixture. Do not prepare batter ahead of time.

Quickly fry each hotcake on a 380° griddle. Each one should be at least 3 inches in diameter.

Serve hotcakes immediately. Top each one with 1 teaspoon sour cream and 1 teaspoon of your favorite jam.

4 servings

Experience a quiet retreat at the *Log Castle Bed and Breakfast Inn* owned by Norma and Jack Metcalf. Their family settled here in 1928 and the lodge was built with materials found on the property. Rough hewn logs, beach stones, and driftwood make up many of the features of the house. The secluded beach offers a panoramic view of Mt. Baker and the grand Cascade mountains.

Raspberry Lemonade Drink

1 (10 ounce) package frozen raspberries in syrup, thawed or 4 cups fresh raspberries
2 cups chilled lemonade

Purée the raspberries in a blender until smooth. Press the purée through a sieve into a bowl to extract all juice; discard seeds.

In a pitcher combine the raspberry juice with the lemonade; chill. Pour the drink over ice cubes in tall glasses and garnish with a lemon twist.

6 servings

Quench your thirst with this refreshing beverage created by Mick and Christy Heggenes at *Christy's Country Inn* near Langley.

Meme's Waffles

2 eggs, separated
1 teaspoon sugar
1/4 cup melted butter
1 1/3 cups flour
1/2 teaspoon salt
2 teaspoons baking powder
1 cup milk

Preheat waffle iron.

In a small bowl, beat egg whites until stiff and set aside. In a large mixing bowl, beat egg yolks until they're lemon colored and foamy. Add sugar and butter and mix well.

In another bowl, sift flour, salt and baking powder together. Alternately add dry ingredients and milk to egg mixture. Fold in beaten egg whites.

Pour 1/2 cup batter onto the waffle iron and cook until golden brown.

Serve waffles hot off the iron. Top with butter and warmed maple syrup.

6 servings

Sunday brunch at Meme's is always a special treat. The unmistakable scent of our favorite airy waffles welcomes us to her cozy home. The table is adorned with pastel flowers, candles, platters of honey baked ham and fresh, juicy fruit.

Try using our recipe for SPICY BUTTER on the waffles. Or, treat your children to a few chocolate chips sprinkled in the batter!

French Toast Decadence

6 eggs
1/2 cup orange juice
1/3 cup orange liqueur
1/2 cup half and half
1 teaspoon vanilla
1/4 teaspoon salt
grated peel of 1 orange
1 loaf cinnamon bread, sliced
4 tablespoons butter

Maple Rum Syrup

Impress your guests with French toast brimming with the flavors of cinnamon and orange. Served with Maple Rum Syrup, this all-time favorite becomes truly decadent.

The night before serving, beat the eggs in a large mixing bowl. Add orange juice, liqueur, half and half, vanilla, salt and orange peel. Mix well. Dip the sliced bread in the egg mixture and place the bread in a baking dish. Cover the dish with plastic wrap and refrigerate overnight.

To prepare the French toast, melt 1 tablespoon butter in a skillet. Brown the soaked bread on both sides. Continue with all pieces. Serve with Maple Rum Syrup.

Maple Rum Syrup

1 cup maple syrup
1 cup honey
2 tablespoons dark rum

In a small saucepan heat the syrup, honey and rum over low heat. Pour warmed syrup into a small pitcher to be poured over individual servings of French toast.

6 servings

Cinnamon Rolls

2 packages dry yeast
1 cup milk, scalded
1/4 cup shortening
1/4 cup sugar
1 teaspoon salt
1 beaten egg
3 1/4 cups flour
1 cup brown sugar

2 tablespoons Karo syrup
2 tablespoons butter

Cinnamon Filling:
3 tablespoons melted butter
1/2 cup brown sugar
1 1/2 teaspoons cinnamon
1/2 cup raisins

Pamper your family with this delicious pastry. Few things are more delightful than waking up to the aroma of freshly baked cinnamon rolls and hot coffee.

This recipe creates a sticky, sweet topping on the buns as opposed to a traditional frosting.

Soften yeast in 1/4 cup warm water, then set aside.

In a large mixing bowl, combine milk, shortening, sugar and salt. Cool until lukewarm. Add yeast and beaten egg to the milk mixture. Gradually mix in flour and beat vigorously to form soft dough. Cover the dough and let it rise in a warm place until double in size.

Place brown sugar, Karo syrup and butter in a 9 x 13-inch baking pan and melt slowly in a warm oven. Remove from oven when melted and spread evenly with a spatula.

Turn the dough out onto a lightly floured surface and knead into a soft roll. Stretch and roll dough out to an 8 x 15-inch rectangle. Brush with 3 tablespoons melted butter and sprinkle the Cinnamon Filling ingredients evenly over the dough. Roll and cut to desired size.

Place rolls in the 9 x 13-inch pan. Cover and let rise in a warm place until the dough has doubled in size.

Preheat oven to 375°.

Bake at 375° for 25 minutes. Cool briefly. Turn pan of rolls onto a surface covered with waxed paper. Drizzle Karo syrup mixture, from the baking pan, over the Cinnamon Rolls.

Serve warm.

1 dozen

Danish Pastry

1 cup flour
1/2 cup margarine

To make the crust, combine the above ingredients with
2 tablespoons water in an electric mixer to form a soft ball.
Divide dough in half. Roll each half to a 4 x 12-inch long
rectangle on an ungreased cookie sheet.

1/2 cup margarine
1 teaspoon almond extract
1 cup flour
3 eggs
slivered almonds for garnish

Preheat oven to 350°.

In a medium saucepan, bring 1 cup water, margarine and almond
extract to a boil over high heat. Remove from heat; and
immediately pour in flour. Stir vigorously until flour is
completely incorporated.

Add eggs to flour mixture, one at a time. When dough is smooth
and shiny, spread over the crust. Bake at 350° for 1 hour. Allow
to cool.

Drizzle your favorite white icing over the pastry and sprinkle
slivered almonds on top. Cut the Danish Pastry into diagonal
strips, arrange on a platter and serve.

16 servings

Any pastry is best when
served soon after baking, and
this recipe is no exception. This
is a fanciful pastry laced with
almond flavoring and drizzled
with a white icing.

*Pastry making was developed
hundreds of year ago in Norman
England. A water and flour paste
was created to form around meats
to prevent it from drying out
during cooking. Pastry making
reached a peak of popularity during
Victorian times.*

Butterhorns

1/2 pound butter
2 cups flour
2/3 cup sour cream
1 egg, separated
3/4 cup sugar
3/4 cup chopped walnuts

Mix butter, flour, sour cream and egg yolk together, reserving egg white. Refrigerate dough for 2 hours.

Divide chilled dough into 4 parts. On a floured surface, roll 1 portion at a time forming a large circle that is 1/4-inch thick. Cut rolled dough into 6 wedges.

Combine sugar and walnuts. Spread each wedge with 1 tablespoon sugar and walnut mixture. Beginning with wide end of wedge, roll it into a crescent shape. Place on an ungreased cookie sheet.

Preheat oven to 350°.

When all Butterhorns have been rolled, brush them with slightly beaten egg white. Sprinkle tops of horns with remaining sugar and walnut mixture.

Bake Butterhorns at 350° for 20 minutes. They freeze beautifully, so make a double batch!

2 dozen

This petite pastry accents any late morning brunch or afternoon tea.

"There are few hours in life more agreeable than afternoon tea."

– Henry James

The Neil Tower and Mt. Baker
Oak Harbor

Maxwelton Fourth of July

South Whidbey's Maxwelton has celebrated the Fourth of July in style for more than 80 years. The annual parade is brimming with participants in costume, on local floats, and vehicles of every kind from tractors to tricycles. The patriotic parade ends at Dave Mackie Memorial Park with a flag-raising ceremony. The afternoon is filled with old-fashioned fun for families, friends and visitors at picnics on the beach and park grounds.

Stuffed Cheese Puffs

Dungeness Crab with Assorted Butters

Beer Bread

Saratoga Summer Salad

Captain Whidbey Chocolate Ice Cream

Snow Cap Cookies

Holmes Harbor Summer Regatta

Colorful sails flap in the breezes of South Whidbey during the Holmes Harbor Regatta. The community of Freeland warmly welcomes sailors and visitors to their summer event. In addition to the sailing fun there are other activities to be enjoyed such as an antique show, a sand castle contest, live music, milk carton races and more.

Pepper Jelly Pinwheels

Artichoke Chicken Manicotti with Fresh Tomato Sauce

Dilled Shrimp Salad

Sourdough Rolls

Rum Soaked Cherries over Vanilla Ice Cream

Hazelnut Truffles

Fresh Fruit Chutney

10 cups sliced fruit: pears, peaches or Italian plums

1/2 cup finely chopped green pepper

1 1/2 cups raisins

4 cups sugar

1 cup chopped crystalized ginger

3 cups vinegar

1/2 teaspoon salt

1/2 teaspoon whole cloves

1/2 teaspoon whole allspice

3 cinnamon sticks

Preheat oven to 350°.

Place all ingredients, except cloves, allspice and cinnamon, in a large roasting pan. Stir gently to blend. Tie the remaining 3 spices together in a piece of cheesecloth. Add to the fruit mixture. Place pan in the oven at 325° until the mixture begins to bubble; approximately 2 hours.

Reduce heat to 200° and bake fruit mixture until dark and thick in consistency; approximately 4 to 5 hours. Stir occasionally.

Ladle Fruit Chutney into hot sterile jars and place hot rings and lids on tops. To assure sealing, place jars in a hot bath for 20 minutes.

Yield: 4 pints

Lois Mitchell's favorite fruit to use in preparing Fruit Chutney is the abundant Whidbey Island Italian plum. The chutney may be served in a small dish to accompany meat, or drizzled over cream cheese to be eaten with crackers.

Crystalized ginger is available in the Oriental section of food markets.

Bell's No-Cook Freezer Jam

1 3/4 quarts fully ripe strawberries
1 3/4 cups sugar
1 package Sure-jell Light Fruit Pectin
1 cup light corn syrup

Wash, hull and thoroughly crush strawberries, one layer at a time. Measure 4 cups berries into a large bowl.

In a small dish containing 1/4 cup of the sugar, add pectin and mix.

Gradually add pectin mixture to fruit, stirring vigorously. Set aside for 30 minutes, stirring occasionally. Add corn syrup; mix well. Gradually stir in remaining sugar until dissolved. Ladle quickly into scalded containers. Cover at once with tight lids.

Let jam stand overnight, then store in freezer. Small amounts may be covered and stored in refrigerator up to 3 weeks.

6 pints

Folks on the north end of Whidbey Island wait patiently through May and June for the opening of the Bell Brothers' berry fields. Strawberries grown on this farm are true "Puget Beauties" – large, deep red and juicy. We have fun picking our own, but you can spoil yourself and have the Bells do it for you!

Pepper Jelly

6 green peppers, quartered

5-7 jalapeño peppers, with or without seeds

3 cups vinegar

12 cups sugar (5 pounds plus 1 cup)

1 teaspoon salt

2 (6 ounce) bottles Certo

green food coloring

2 blocks paraffin wax

Combine all peppers and 1/2 cup vinegar in a blender or food processor. Mix until it is puréed. Place pepper mixture in the bottom of a large stock pot or a 6 to 8-quart pot. Add sugar, remaining 2 1/2 cups vinegar, and salt. Bring to a boil and boil mixture for 3 minutes to dissolve sugar. Add Certo to pepper mixture and boil 1 minute more. Sprinkle in a few drops of food coloring to desired coloring.

Place Pepper Jelly in hot jars and cover with melted paraffin to seal. Or, ladle the Pepper Jelly into hot sterile jars and place hot rings and lids on top. To assure sealing, place jars in a hot bath for 20 minutes.

6 pints

Lois Mitchell urges her friends to sample her Pepper Jelly. She finds that most people are intrigued by its vibrant color, as well as the taste. The jelly is wonderful drizzled over a block of cream cheese and served with crackers.

Lois creates Pepper Jelly Pinwheels by whipping 1 part pepper jelly with 3 parts cream cheese. Spread it over lefse, a Norwegian flatbread. Lay thin slices of salami on top. Roll as you would in making a jellyroll; chill and slice.

Southern Blueberry Barbeque Sauce

1 tablespoon olive oil

1/2 yellow onion, pared and diced

2 cloves crushed garlic

1/4 cup red Zinfandel wine

1/2 cup cider vinegar

2 1/2 pounds of fresh or frozen blueberries

1/4 cup brown sugar

1 tablespoon worcestershire sauce

juice of 1 lemon

1/16 teaspoon red pepper flakes

1/16 teaspoon chili powder

salt and pepper to taste

In a large saucepan or stock pot, heat oil over medium heat. Add the onion and garlic and sauté until translucent, but not brown. Add wine and vinegar and bring ingredients to simmering point. Add blueberries, brown sugar, worcestershire, lemon and all seasonings. Bring the mixture back to the simmering point. Cook over low heat until the sauce begins to thicken. This takes approximately 2 hours.

When the sauce has thickened, pour it into a food processor or blender and purée. Taste and adjust the seasoning if necessary.

Store your Blueberry Barbeque Sauce in a tightly covered container or glass jars. When it is time to barbeque, baste fish or chicken entreés with the sauce.

Yield: 1 quart

Julie Wilson acquired this recipe from her grandmother, a long time resident of the heart of Alabama. The combination of such unusual flavors creates a barbeque sauce that is absolutely unique. Store it in the refrigerator to baste on fish or chicken.

BBQ Sauce

1/4 cup worcestershire
1/4 cup liquid smoke
1/2 cup chili powder
1 1/2 cups water
3 1/2 (32 ounce) jars
  ketchup

1/4 cup vinegar
1 pound light brown
  sugar
1/4 cup tabasco
1 tablespoon garlic
  powder

We use Van Westfall's
barbeque sauce all year long.

Mix all ingredients in a large pot. Bring to a boil; then lower heat
and simmer for 3 hours.

Store in refrigerator or freeze for several months.

Yield: 4 quarts

Sweet and Sour Stir-Fry Sauce

8 cloves garlic, minced
1/3 cup minced fresh
  ginger
1 1/2 cups water
1/3 cup soy sauce
1 cup vinegar

1/3 cup sherry
1/4 cup catsup
1 cup sugar
3 tablespoons sesame oil
1/2 teaspoon hot red
  pepper flakes

This spicy sauce is not for
the timid.

Combine all ingredients in a jar with a tight fitting lid. Shake
well and chill up to 3 weeks.

Before serving, shake jar of sauce well. Mix 1 cup sauce with
1 tablespoon cornstarch and pour over pan of stir-fried meat,
poultry or shrimp and thinly sliced vegetables. Stir over high
heat to boiling.

Yield: 4 cups

Fresh Tomato Sauce

2 pounds ripe tomatoes
1 cup finely chopped onion
4 cloves garlic, minced
1/4 cup olive oil
1 teaspoon salt
1/2 teaspoon pepper
3 leaves fresh basil
3 tablespoons tomato paste

Peel, seed and chop fresh tomatoes.

In a deep saucepan, sauté onion and garlic in the oil until golden. Add tomatoes and cook over medium heat for 10 minutes, stirring occasionally. Add the seasonings and tomato paste and let the sauce cook for 5 minutes more.

Pour into sterile jars, seal and refrigerate. Tomato sauce may be frozen for 2 to 4 months.

Yield: 1 1/2 pints

After defrosting the Fresh Tomato Sauce, plan to taste and season it again since seasonings lose their strength in the freezer. Tomato sauce can also be used as the base for a delightful instant soup. Simply defrost and heat the sauce. Put it through a food mill, add CHICKEN STOCK or water, and a bit of milk to desired consistency. Serve warm.

Fresh vine ripened tomatoes and fresh basil make this tomato sauce extraordinary. We use it for all of our pasta dishes that call for tomato sauce.

Sun Dried Tomatoes

small Roma or cherry tomatoes

coarse salt (such as Margarita salt)

vinegar

extra virgin olive oil

fresh rosemary, basil or thyme leaves (optional)

fresh garlic, peeled (optional)

Preheat oven to 200°.

Cut small tomatoes into quarters or cherry tomatoes in half. Arrange the tomato pieces, cut side up, on a baking sheet. Sprinkle with salt. Place the baking sheet in the oven for 5 to 7 hours. Watch tomatoes carefully after 5 hours to make sure they do not burn.

When pieces dry completely, they should have a dried, shriveled appearance. As individual pieces dry completely, remove them, dip each one in vinegar, and layer in a sterile glass jar. Cover the tomatoes completely with olive oil. Add optional herbs or garlic if desired.

These tomatoes will last for months in or out of the refrigerator, or can be frozen.

Carol Dearth raises a garden full of Roma and cherry tomatoes to be used each year as Sun Dried Tomatoes. They are fun to use in Italian foccacia bread, pizza dough or in the pizza topping. They are also great on top of salads. The possibilities are endless, so try making them and add a splash of color to your meals.

Basil, a tropical member of the mint family, is originally from India. It did not reach western Europe until the 16th century. This herb has a spicy scent and flavor with a hint of mint and cloves. Basil blends well with garlic and lemon. It is best when used fresh or kept in a jar with olive oil and a little salt. The white blooms of basil are lovely on vegetables and salads.

Marinated Carrots

1 pound carrots, peeled	1/2 teaspoon mustard seed
2 whole bay leaves	1/2 teaspoon dill weed
1/2 cup white wine vinegar	1/4 teaspoon crushed red pepper
2 tablespoons sugar	1/4 teaspoon dill seed
1/2 teaspoon salt	1 clove garlic, minced

Cut peeled carrots into fourths and desired length. Arrange them in a vegetable steamer basket in a large pan. Cook carrots over medium high heat for 10 minutes until barely tender. Remove from high heat and plunge into a pan of cold water, then drain.

Pack carrots with bay leaves in a glass jar. In a small bowl, mix all spices with vinegar, sugar and garlic. Stir well until sugar is dissolved. Pour mixture over the carrots and cover tightly.

Refrigerate Marinated Carrots for at least 2 days to allow the flavors a chance to blend and be absorbed. The carrots will keep in the refrigerator for up to 3 weeks.

Yield: 1 pound carrots

Packed in a jar with a brightly colored ribbon, these crisp and highly seasoned carrots will make a perfect gift from your kitchen.

Dried Bouquet Garni

4 bay leaves, broken	4 teaspoons dried rosemary
4 tablespoons dried tarragon	4 teaspoons dried thyme
4 tablespoons dried parsley	

Combine the herbs. Cut a double layer of cheesecloth into 8 4-inch squares. Put 1 tablespoon of herb mixture in the center of each square. Gather the edges of the cheesecloth together to form a small bag and tie with kitchen twine or heavy thread. They will resemble small sachets.

Place in a decorative jar or container and tie with a bright ribbon.

Yield: 8 bundles

Bouquet Garni is a combination of herbs used to flavor dishes as they cook. Drop a bundle into stews, soups or simmering meats.

Assorted Vinegars

Berry Vinegar

1 pound fresh raspberries or blackberries, cleaned
1/4 cup sugar
3/4 cup white vinegar
1/4 cup red wine

Sprinkle berries with sugar and allow to set for 1 hour until juices form. Combine all ingredients in a medium saucepan and bring to a boil. Cook for 5 minutes and pour into a clean, hot jar.

Store vinegar for 2 weeks in a cool, dark spot. After 2 weeks strain vinegar through cheesecloth pressing juice from berries. Discard berries and pour vinegar into a clean hot jar and seal.

Yield: 1 1/2 cups

Tarragon Garlic Vinegar

1 1/2 cups white vinegar
1/2 cup white wine
2 cloves garlic, halved
3 sprigs fresh tarragon

Combine vinegar and wine and pour into jars. Add garlic and fresh tarragon to each jar. Place on rack in large pot of water and heat to boiling. Allow to cool. Seal and store in a cool, dark place for 2 weeks.

Yield: 1 pint

Basil Red Wine Vinegar

1 1/2 cups white vinegar
1/2 cup dry red wine
1 leafy sprig fresh basil

Combine vinegar and wine and pour into jar. Add basil sprig. Place on rack in large pot of water and heat to boiling. Allow to cool. Seal and store in a cool, dark place for 2 weeks.

Yield: 1 pint

Homemade vinegar is a great "hostess" gift. It's a fun opportunity to be creative in your kitchen and experiment with different combinations of herbs, spices and fruit. These vinegars are terrific in salad dressings or sprinkled over fresh vegetables.

Before beginning your vinegar production, collect a number of fancy, long-necked bottles in which to store your end result.

Try sealing the filled bottles by closing tightly and dipping the lid in melted paraffin to which 1 teaspoon cinnamon has been added. Design your own label and finish with a ribbon.

Herbed Beef Jerky

1 to 1 1/2 pounds boneless beef top round,
    partially frozen
2 cloves garlic, minced
3/4 cup deep red wine
1 tablespoon thyme leaves
2 whole bay leaves
1 teaspoon salt
1 teaspoon worcestershire
1 1/2 teaspoons marjoram
1/4 teaspoon pepper

Trim and discard all fat from the beef. Slice the meat 1/8 inch
thick and as long as possible. Set aside.

Combine garlic, wine and all spices in a saucepan. Simmer over
low heat for 5 minutes. Remove from heat, transfer to a bowl
and cool.

Marinate the meat strips in the herbed wine, marking sure all
meat is covered. Tightly cover the bowl and marinate several
hours or overnight.

Blot off all liquid from meat. Arrange strips (without
overlapping), in 2 foil lined 9 x 13-inch pans. Dry meat in a
200° oven for 5-6 hours, or until the meat has turned dark brown
and feels dry. Blot again if necessary. Allow meat to cool before
removing from pans.

Store Herbed Beef Jerky in tightly covered containers at room
temperature. It will stay fresh for a very long time.

Yield: 8 ounces Beef Jerky

Keep this jerky on hand for
nutritional snacks or lunch time
treats.

*If you substitute dried for fresh
herbs, do so sparingly. Dried herbs
do not keep their aroma much
longer than a year, so buy them in
small amounts. We encourage you
to grow your own fresh herbs.
They require well drained soil and
sunlight which helps in developing
their volatile oils. The oils produce
the plant's characteristic scent and
flavor.*

Savory Sausage

6 pounds ground lean beef
5 teaspoons cured salt
2 1/2 tablespoons mustard seed

2 1/2 teaspoons course
    ground pepper
2 1/2 teaspoons garlic salt
3 teaspoons liquid smoke

In a large mixing bowl, blend all ingredients thoroughly with your hands. Cover tightly and refrigerate beef for 2 days. On the third day, remove beef from the refrigerator and form it into 6 equal parts. On a piece of waxed paper pat each part into a sausage roll shape.

Preheat oven to 150°.

Place each sausage roll on the rack of a broiler pan. Allow the fat to drip into the bottom half of the pan. Place the broiler pan with sausage on the lowest rack of your oven. Bake at 150° for 8 hours, turning sausage every 2 hours. Remove sausage from the oven and wrap each roll tightly in foil.

Savory Sausage may be stored in the refrigerator for several weeks, however, it should be frozen for longer storage.

6 (1 pound) rolls

A tasty holiday gift to make for your friends and neighbors.

Papa's Special Seasoning

3 (11 1/2 ounce) jars garlic powder
3 (11 1/2 ounce) jars garlic salt
2 pounds salt
3 (2 1/4 ounce) jars unsalted "Adolph's" meat tenderizer
7 (1/2 ounce) jars oregano
pepper to taste

Mix all ingredients together in a large bowl. Store in seasoning bottles or tins.

Glen Weaver used this simple combination of spices to provide a surprisingly new dimension to any meat, fish or vegetable.

To prolong the life of any spice it is recommended that they are properly sealed and stored away from heat sources. In fact, refrigeration is ideal.

Chocolate Cream Cups

1/3 cup (2 ounces) coarsely chopped semi-sweet
  chocolate
14 (1 inch) foil candy cups or 24 (1 1/2 inch) paper
  candy cups

Melt chocolate in a double boiler over simmering heat. Stir
often until chocolate is melted. Remove from heat.

With a 1/4 inch wide paint brush paint chocolate into foil or
paper cases. If using paper cases stack 2 or 3 cases for added
strength. After painting 1 coat, chill in refrigerator until the
chocolate is hard.

Paint another layer of chocolate onto chocolate filled cases.
The sides and bottom of the cup should be approximately
1/8 inch thick. Chill in refrigerator again until chocolate is
hard, about 15 minutes.

The chocolate cups can be stored in the refrigerator for up to
3 weeks in an airtight container.

Before using, carefully peel away foil or paper casings without
touching chocolate, as the heat from your hands may melt the
chocolate.

Using a small spoon fill chocolate cups with sweetened, whipped
cream or the liqueur of your choice. Drop one cup into your
espresso and pop another into your mouth.

14-24 cups

The casings used to form
these chocolate cups can be
found in the cake decorating
section of cookware stores.

*In 1828, an Amsterdam
confectioner, Conrad van
Houten, made a screw press to
force the vegetable oils (cocoa
butter) out of cocoa. The result
was cocoa powder that could be
reduced to fine granules and
mixed with sugar, creating
"Dutch chocolate."*

Rum Soaked Cherries

3 pounds large cherries, pitted
6 cups sugar
1 quart rum (approximate)

Place cherries in a large pan and cover with sugar. Let them stand one hour until juices form. Cook slowly over low heat for 20 minutes.

Remove the fruit from syrup and continue to cook syrup until it is slightly thickened. Measure syrup and add 1/4 cup rum for every cup of syrup. Pour rum syrup over cherries and seal the mixture at once by placing it in hot, sterilized jars.

Yield: 4 cups

Prepare this recipe in the summer, when the cherries are fresh. Allow them to marinate for several months. Serve the Rum Soaked Cherries over ice cream or pound cake.

Vanilla Extract

2 vanilla beans
1 pint brandy

Slice the vanilla beans down the center to expose the vanilla seeds. Drop them into a bottle of brandy. Shake the bottle, cover and allow beans to marinate in the brandy for 4 weeks before using. Shake the mixture every few days.

Remove the beans from the brandy and discard.

Pour your vanilla extract into smaller bottles and cap. Tie a ribbon around those you are using for gifts and don't forget to keep some to enjoy using yourself.

Yield: 2 cups

True vanilla extract is easily discernible from the imitation variety. The extract is so easy to make that we urge you to try it.

The vanilla bean looks like a slender, deep brown stick about 6 inches long. The bean is actually the fruit of a lovely climbing orchid. Most vanilla beans come from Madagascar.

Chocolate Coconut Drops

1 cup sweetened condensed milk
1 (12 ounce) bag coconut
1 pound powdered sugar
2 cups chopped pecans
1/4 pound margarine, melted
1/2 bar paraffin wax
1 (12 ounce) bag semi-sweet chocolate chips

In a large bowl, mix together sweetened milk, coconut and sugar. Blend in nuts and margarine. Using a small spoon, drop candy pieces on to a cookie sheet. Cool in the refrigerator for 1 hour.

In the top of a double boiler saucepan, melt the paraffin and chocolate chips over low heat. Stir well. Roll each candy piece into a ball. Dip balls into the chocolate, one at a time, and place on waxed paper to set.

36 pieces

Enjoy this sweet confection from Julie Morgan's kitchen. Sweet coconut gently dipped in chocolate is a delightful combination.

We have discovered that one of the best ways to evenly dip candy is by placing each piece on the end of a wooden kabob stick and rolling the candy in the chocolate.

Amaretto Cream

1 (14 ounce) can sweetened condensed milk
1 3/4 cup Amaretto
4 eggs
1 teaspoon instant coffee granules
2 teaspoons almond extract
2 teaspoons vanilla extract
1 cup heavy cream

Combine all ingredients together in a blender. Process until they are thoroughly blended and smooth. Store in a tightly capped bottle or bottles.

Amaretto Cream should be consumed within 30 days of the day it is made. Store it in a refrigerator.

Yield: 4 cups

Kay Anderson has created something "strictly adult." We urge you to try this rich and creamy almond flavored dessert drink. Make a batch of Amaretto Cream to give to your friends.

Hazelnut Truffles

1 cup shelled and skinned hazelnut filberts

3/4 cup butter, melted

3 ounces semi-sweet chocolate

3 ounces milk chocolate

5 egg yolks

1 cup powdered sugar

1 teaspoon vanilla

1 cup chocolate sprinkles or finely chopped nuts

Chop the hazelnuts in a food processor or electric blender. Add 6 tablespoons of the melted butter. Whirl until the mixture is smooth and creamy.

Add the chocolate to the remaining 6 tablespoons butter in a small saucepan. Stir until the chocolate is melted and the mixture is smooth.

In a large bowl beat the egg yolks with an electric mixer until they are foamy. Gradually add sugar and continue beating; add vanilla.

Add nut butter one tablespoon at a time, beating after each addition. Add chocolate very slowly while mixer continues to run. When the mixture is smooth and well blended cover the bowl and chill for 30 minutes.

Put the chocolate sprinkles or chopped nuts in a small bowl. Form rounded teaspoonfuls of the truffle mixture into balls and roll in sprinkles or nuts.

Place truffles in small paper cups and arrange in a tin. These may be refrigerated for up to 2 weeks or frozen for a month.

36 pieces

These creamy fudge confections are quick to make yet elegantly impressive.

In 1847, Fry and Sons of London made the first eating chocolate.

Sugared Walnuts

2 1/2 cups shelled walnuts
1 tablespoon butter
1 cup sugar
1 teaspoon cinnamon
1/2 teaspoon salt
1/2 teaspoon vanilla

Preheat oven to 375°.

Spread walnuts out on a cookie sheet. Warm walnuts in the oven for 5 minutes. Remove from oven and cover to keep warm.

Butter the sides of a 2-quart saucepan. Combine sugar, 1/2 cup water, cinnamon and salt in the pan and cook over medium high heat, without stirring. Using a candy thermometer, bring the mixture to "soft ball" stage. Immediately remove from heat when this occurs.

Using a hand mixer or a wire whip, beat the mixture for 1 minute until smooth and creamy. Add vanilla and stir to blend.

Place the nuts on a sheet of waxed paper. Pour the sugar mixture over warm nuts and allow to cool.

Store the nuts in a tightly covered container.

Yield: 2 1/2 cups walnuts

A holiday treat in Jean Lange's home is Sugared Walnuts. She also makes them as a gift for friends.

You may want a 6-inch circle of holiday fabric to place under a jar lid; forming a ruffle. Label your jar of sugared walnuts to let your friends know they were "homemade" by you.

Caramel Popcorn

5 quarts popped corn, or 3 packages microwave popcorn
1 cup butter
2 cups brown sugar
1/2 cup corn syrup
1 teaspoon salt
1 teaspoon vanilla
1/2 teaspoon soda
peanuts, optional

Over medium high heat melt butter, brown sugar, corn syrup and salt. Stirring constantly, bring mixture to a boil. Allow the mixture to boil for 5 minutes without stirring. Remove from heat and add vanilla and soda. Mix thoroughly.

Preheat oven to 250°.

Evenly distribute the popped corn on 2 ungreased cookie sheets. Pour the caramel over the popped corn. Add peanuts, if desired.

Bake in a 250° oven, on the 2 center racks, for 1 hour. Stir and turn through the popcorn every 15 minutes.

Remove from oven while warm and immediately lay the popcorn on sheets of waxed paper. You may wish to break the popcorn into smaller chunks.

Yield: 5 quarts

Caramel coated popcorn is an appealing treat to children and adults. Chira Flowers' crisp, full flavored caramel popcorn is great to give as a gift . . . that is, if it lasts long enough to make it out of the kitchen! Make it for parties and watch it disappear before your eyes. Be sure to store it in an airtight tin or a sealed freezer bag.

Natural Dyed Easter Eggs

2 cups packed onion skins from red and brown onions
fresh herbs and greens
1 dozen eggs
1 tablespoon oil

Place onion skins in a large pot of boiling water. Allow skins to boil while preparing eggs.

Rip old pieces of cloth into squares approximately 4 inches on each side. Place some herbs and greens on each square. Place an egg in the middle of the square on top of the greens. Wrap the cloth around the egg making sure that some herbs or greens are pressing against all surfaces of the egg. Wrap cloth covered egg gently but firmly with string or heavy thread.

Carefully lower eggs into pot of boiling water and onion skins. Allow to boil for 15 minutes. Drain eggs and flush with cold water. Untie the strings and remove wrapping and herbs from eggs. Rinse and pat dry. You should see the imprint of the herbs at this point.

Rubbing hard boiled eggs with a bit of oil makes them shiny. Place in a basket of grass and wrap the basket with a pastel ribbon.

12 eggs

Create Easter eggs in the "country French" tradition. They will make an unusual springtime decoration or gift from all natural ingredients. The imprint from the fresh herbs will be visible on the light brown eggs.

"Take time to listen and talk about the voices of the earth and what they mean – the majestic voice of thunder, the winds, the sound of surf or flowing streams."

– Rachel Carson

Front Street
Coupeville

Tourist Information

Washington State Park information
1-800-562-0990

Island Transit
206-678-7771

Washington State Ferry
1-800-542-7052

Oak Harbor Marina
206-679-2628

Coupeville Harbormaster
206-678-5020

Langley Marina
206-321-5945

Port of South Whidbey
206-321-5494

Central Whidbey Chamber of Commerce
206-678-5434

Clinton Chamber of Commerce
206-321-6455

Langley Chamber of Commerce
206-321-6765

Freeland Chamber of Commerce
206-321-1980

Oak Harbor Chamber of Commerce
206-675-3535

Island County Historical Museum
206-678-3310

Red Tide Hotline
1-800-562-5632

Whale Watcher's Hotline
1-800-562-8832

For more information on the history of Whidbey Island, see Jimmie Jean Cook's *A Favorite Friend, Penn Cove*; Kellogg's *History of Whidbey Island*; or Dorothy Neil's book *By Canoe and Sailing Ship They Came*.

Almond Bars	166
AMARETTO	
Amaretto Alarms	147
Amaretto Cream	214
Victorian Amaretto Cheese Dip	156
APPETIZERS	
Appetizing Mini Quiches	22
Bacon Stuffed Mushrooms	28
Beef Teriyaki	21
Button Mushroom Dip	27
Cheddar Asparagus Roll-Ups	25
Clams on the Half Shell	17
Continental Cheese Fondue	29
Crab Deviled Eggs	19
Creamy Garlic Cheese	24
Escargot in Mushroom Caps	18
Fiesta Bean Dip	32
Guacamole Dip	33
Hot Artichoke Spread	31
Pita Chips	31
Seabolt's Smoked Salmon Antipasto	14
Seabolt's Smoked Salmon Pâté	14
Smoked Salmon and Onion Cheesecake	13
Spicy Chile Cheese Squares	23
Spinach Turnovers	26
Steak Tartare	20
Stuffed Cheese Puffs	24
Taco Salsa	33
Turkish Fried Mussels	16
Vegetable Cheese Spread	30
Warm Crab Dip	19
Whidbey Fish Mussels	15
ARTICHOKES	
Artichoke Caesar Salad	52
Artichoke Chicken Manicotti	98
Artichokes with Dips	80
Hot Artichoke Spread	31
ASPARAGUS	
Asparagus with Raspberry Mousseline	79
Cheddar Asparagus Roll-Ups	25
Springtime Asparagus	79
Tarragon Asparagus	57
AVOCADO	
Avocado with Honeycream Dressing	62
Guacamole Dip	33
Bacon Stuffed Mushrooms	28
Banana Cake with Whipped Cream Frosting	162
BARBEQUE	
Barbeque Sauce	205
Barbequed Salmon in Citrus and Wine	118
Southern Blueberry Barbeque Sauce	204
BEANS	
Fiesta Bean Dip	32
Red Beans and Rice	101
Rockwell Baked Beans	81
BEEF	
Beef Fondue with Assorted Sauces	110
Beef Jerky	210
Beef Stock	39
Beef Teriyaki	21
Mexican Curry	107
Oyster Sauce Beef	109
Pacific Flank Steak	111
Paruskys	103
Savory Sausage	211
Spud Stew	106
Steak Tartare	20
Stuffed Burgers	105
Tex Mex Enchiladas	108
BEVERAGES	
Egg Nog	34
Hot Buttered Rum	34
Orange Frappé	191
Raspberry Lemonade	193
Sangria	32
BLUEBERRIES	
Blueberry Cream Cheese Crepes	143
Southern Blueberry Barbeque Sauce	204
BREADS	
Baguettes	180
Banana Bread	176
Beach House Lemon Bread	175
Beer Bread	178
Butterhorns	198
Carrot Pineapple Bread	174
Cinnamon Rolls	196
Coconut Date Muffins	171
Dilly Bread	177
Dutch Rye Bread	178
Four Seed Crunchy Bread	179
Oatmeal Squash Bread	173
Pita Chips	31

Refrigerator Bran Muffins	172
Yeast Rolls	181

BROCCOLI

Broccoli Casserole	82
Broccoli with Lemon Herb Sauce	83
Cream of Broccoli Soup	46

BRUNCH

Breakfast Parfait	186
Chocolate Dipped Strawberries	184
Cottage Cheese Hot Cakes	193
Country Cottage Breakfast	186
Danish Pastry	197
Eagle's Nest Zesty Eggs	187
Eggs Portugal	188
French Toast Decadence	195
Fruits Gourmands	183
Hot Baked Fruit	185
Island Pears	185
Meme's Waffles	194
Potato Torte	192
San de Fuca Eggs	189
Smoked Salmon Scrambled Eggs	191
Souffle Pillars	190
Strawberries Devonshire	184
Brussels Sprouts and Onions in Savory Wine Sauce	74

BUTTERS

Anchovy Butter	126
French Herb Butter	182
Honey Butter	182
Lemon and Caper Butter	126
Onion Butter	126
Soy Sauce Butter	126
Spicy Butter	182

CAKE

Banana Cake with Whipped Cream Frosting	162
Chocolate Espresso Cake	153
Chocolate Lover's Cake	154
Fresh Fruit and Cream Cake	161
Italian Cream Cake	163
Washington Apple Cake	160

CANDY

Caramel Popcorn	217
Chocolate Coconut Drops	214
Chocolate Cream Cups	212
Hazelnut Truffles	215

CARROTS

Autumn Baked Carrots	73
Glazed Carrots	73
Marinated Carrots	208
Cauliflower Sauté	78

CHEESE

Creamy Garlic Cheese	24
Spicy Chile Cheese Squares	23
Stuffed Cheese Puffs	24
Vegetable Cheese Spread	30

CHEESECAKE

Boudoir Cheesecake	159
Very Best Cheesecake	158
Cherries, Rum Soaked	213

CHICKEN

Artichoke Chicken Manicotti	98
Chicken Loganberry	93
Chicken Parmesan on Pasta	97
Chicken Stock	38
Coq au Vin	95
Curried Chicken Luncheon Salad	58
Norman's Watermark Sandwiches	94
Shanghai Chicken Salad	56
Stuffed Chicken Breasts with Red Wine Sauce	96
Chilies, Spicy Chile Cheese Squares	23
Chowder, Crescent Harbor Clam	41
Chowder, *Whidbey Fish*	131
Chutney, Fresh Fruit Chutney	201
Clams on the Half Shell	17

COCONUT

Chocolate Coconut Drops	214
Coconut Baked Sweet Potatoes	85
Coconut Date Muffins	171
Coffee, Dutch	164

COOKIES

Bears Chocolate Chip Cookies	167
Oatmeal Raisin Cookies	168
Snow Caps	165

COOKIES, BAR

Almond Bars	166
Chocolate Raspberry Meringue	152
Jan Hagel	164
Cornish Game Hens, Glazed	92
Cottage Cheese Hotcakes	193

CRAB

Crab and Shrimp Sandwich	127

Index

Crab Broccoli Bake	128
Dungeness Crab with Butters	126
Warm Crab Dip	19
CREAM	
Amaretto Cream	214
Lime Cream	157
Red Grapes in Sherried Cream	156
Crepes, Blueberry Cream Cheese Crepes	143
DESSERT	
Almond Bars	166
Amaretto Alarms	147
Banana Cake with Whipped Cream Frosting	162
Bears Chocolate Chip Cookies	167
Bell's Strawberry Tart	150
Berry Rhubarb Fool	149
Blueberry Cream Cheese Crepes	143
Boudoir Cheesecake	159
Captain Whidbey Chocolate Ice Cream	146
Chocolate Espresso Cake	153
Chocolate Lover's Cake	154
Chocolate Mousse	155
Chocolate Raspberry Meringue Bars	152
Fresh Berry Pies	142
Fresh Fruit and Cream Cake	161
Frozen Lemon Delight	147
Island Blackberry Cobbler	144
Italian Cream Cake	163
Jan Hagel	164
Lime Cream	157
Loganberry Champagne Spoom	145
Loganberry Sherbet	145
Meringue Lemon Dessert	148
Oatmeal Raisin Cookies	168
Olie Bollen	164
Red Grapes in Sherried Cream	156
Snow Caps	165
Strawberry Delight	150
The Very Best Cheesecake	158
Victorian Amaretto Cheese Dip	156
Washington Apple Cake	160
Whidbey's Berry Pie	141
White Cloud Pie	151
DIPS	
Button Mushroom Dip	27
Curry Dip	80
Fiesta Bean Dip	32
Guacamole	33
DUTCH PASTRIES	
Jan Hagel	164
Olie Bollen	164
Easter Eggs, Natural Dyed	218
Egg Nog	34
ENTRÉES	
Artichoke Chicken Manicotti	98
Baked Ham Basted with Rum	111
Beef Fondue with Sauces	110
Chicken Loganberry	93
Chicken Parmesan on Pasta	97
Coq au Vin	95
Fettucine al Pesto	99
Glazed Cornish Hens	92
Lamb Curry with Fruit	113
Lowell's Dogs	104
Mexican Curry	107
Norman's Watermark Sandwich	94
Oyster Sauce Beef	109
Pacific Flank Steak	111
Parusky	103
Pizza Pattee	102
Pork Chops with Red Apples	112
Rabbit Hunter's Style	91
Red Beans and Rice	101
Spaghetti Alla Amalfitana	100
Spud Stew	106
Stuffed Burgers	105
Stuffed Chicken Breasts with Red Wine Sauce	96
Stuffed Leg of Lamb	114
Tex Mex Enchiladas	108
Escargot in Mushroom Caps	18
GIFTS FROM THE KITCHEN	
Amaretto Cream	214
Assorted Vinegars	209
Barbeque Sauce	205
Bell's No-Cook Freezer Jam	202
Bouquet Garni	208
Caramel Popcorn	217
Chocolate Coconut Drops	214
Chocolate Cream Cups	212
Fresh Fruit Chutney	201
Fresh Tomato Sauce	206
Hazelnut Truffles	215
Herbed Beef Jerky	210

Index

Homemade Vanilla Extract	213
Marinated Carrots	208
Natural Dyed Easter Eggs	218
Papa's Special Seasoning	211
Pepper Jelly	203
Rum Soaked Cherries	213
Savory Sausage	211
Southern Blueberry Barbeque Sauce	204
Sugared Walnuts	216
Sun Dried Tomatoes	207
Sweet and Sour Stir Fry Sauce	205

HALIBUT
Barbequed Halibut	133
Halibut Dijon	134

HAM
Baked Ham Basted with Rum	111
Spaghetti Alla Amalfitana	100
Hotcakes, Cottage Cheese	193
Ice Cream, Captain Whidbey Chocolate	146
Jam, Bell's No-Cook Freezer	202
Jelly, Pepper	203

LEMON
Frozen Lemon Delight	147
Meringue Lemon Dessert	148
Raspberry Lemonade	193

LAMB
Lamb Curry with Fruit	113
Stuffed Leg of Lamb	114

LOGANBERRIES
Chicken Loganberry	93
Loganberry Sherbet	145
Whidbey's Loganberry Champagne Spoom	145
Muffins, Coconut Date	171

MUSHROOMS
Bacon Stuffed	28
Cashew Mushroom Soup	45
Escargot in Mushroom Caps	18

MUSSELS
King Salmon in Champagne Sauce with Penn Cove Mussels	121
Race Lagoon Mussels with Corn and Red Pepper Sauce	122
Stuffed Penn Cove Mussels	123
Turkish Fried Mussels	16
Whidbey Fish Mussels	15
Oatmeal Raisin Cookies	168

ONIONS
Golden Onion Soup	47
Swiss Onion Bake	75

OYSTERS
Oyster Sauce Beef	109
Puget Sound Oyster Bisque	40
Stuffed Olympic Oysters	124

PASTA
Artichoke Chicken Manicotti	98
Chicken Parmesan on Pasta	97
Fettucine al Pesto	99
Peg's Pasta Salad	65
Seafood Pasta	130
Spaghetti Alla Amalfitana	100
Pears, Island	185

PEAS
Purée of Peas	84
Split Pea Soup	43

PIE
Fresh Strawberry Pie	142
Whidbey's Berry Pie	141
White Cloud Pie	151
Pineapple, B's Pineapple Dressing	67
Pizza Pattee	102
Pork Chops with Red Apples	112

POTATOES
Potato Torte	192
Potatoes with Rosemary and Garlic	86
Vichyssoise	49
Potatoes, Coconut Baked Sweet	85
Quiche, Appetizing Mini	22
Rabbit Hunter's Style	91

RASPBERRY
Asparagus with Raspberry Mousseline	79
Fresh Raspberry Pie	142
Raspberry Lemonade Drink	193
Red Snapper, Northwest	138
Rhubarb, Berry Rhubarb Fool	149

RICE
Orange Rice	87
Six Persimmons Fried Rice	88
Smoked Salmon Rice Salad	61
Rum, Hot Buttered	34

SALAD DRESSINGS
B's Pineapple Dressing	67
Blue Cheese Dressing	53